PRIVACY RESEARCH AND BEST PRACTICES

Summary of a Workshop for the Intelligence Community

Emily Grumbling, *Rapporteur*

Computer Science and Telecommunications Board

Division on Engineering and Physical Sciences

The National Academies of
SCIENCES · ENGINEERING · MEDICINE

THE NATIONAL ACADEMIES PRESS
Washington, DC
www.nap.edu

THE NATIONAL ACADEMIES PRESS   500 Fifth Street, NW   Washington, DC 20001

This activity was supported by the Office of the Director of National Intelligence, under Contract No. 2014-14041100003-001. Any opinions, findings, conclusions, or recommendations expressed in this publication do not necessarily reflect the views of any organization or agency that provided support for the project.

International Standard Book Number-13: 978-0-309-38919-8
International Standard Book Number-10: 0-309-38919-4
Digital Object Identifier: 10.17226/21879

Additional copies of this workshop summary are available for sale from the National Academies Press, 500 Fifth Street, NW, Keck 360, Washington, DC 20001; (800) 624-6242 or (202) 334-3313; http://www.nap.edu.

Copyright 2016 by the National Academy of Sciences. All rights reserved.

Printed in the United States of America.

Suggested citation: National Academies of Sciences, Engineering, and Medicine. 2016. *Privacy Research and Best Practices: Summary of a Workshop for the Intelligence Community*. Washington, DC: The National Academies Press. doi:10.17226/21879.

The National Academies of
SCIENCES · ENGINEERING · MEDICINE

The **National Academy of Sciences** was established in 1863 by an Act of Congress, signed by President Lincoln, as a private, nongovernmental institution to advise the nation on issues related to science and technology. Members are elected by their peers for outstanding contributions to research. Dr. Ralph J. Cicerone is president.

The **National Academy of Engineering** was established in 1964 under the charter of the National Academy of Sciences to bring the practices of engineering to advising the nation. Members are elected by their peers for extraordinary contributions to engineering. Dr. C. D. Mote, Jr., is president.

The **National Academy of Medicine** (formerly the Institute of Medicine) was established in 1970 under the charter of the National Academy of Sciences to advise the nation on medical and health issues. Members are elected by their peers for distinguished contributions to medicine and health. Dr. Victor J. Dzau is president.

The three Academies work together as the **National Academies of Sciences, Engineering, and Medicine** to provide independent, objective analysis and advice to the nation and conduct other activities to solve complex problems and inform public policy decisions. The Academies also encourage education and research, recognize outstanding contributions to knowledge, and increase public understanding in matters of science, engineering, and medicine.

Learn more about the National Academies of Sciences, Engineering, and Medicine at **www.national-academies.org.**

Other Recent Reports of the Computer Science and Telecommunications Board

Bulk Collection of Signals Intelligence: Technical Options (2015)
Interim Report on 21st Century Cyber-Physical Systems Education (2015)
A Review of the Next Generation Air Transportation System: Implications and Importance of System Architecture (2015)
Telecommunications Research and Engineering at the Communications Technology Laboratory of the Department of Commerce: Meeting the Nation's Telecommunications Needs (2015)
Telecommunications Research and Engineering at the Institute for Telecommunication Sciences of the Department of Commerce: Meeting the Nation's Telecommunications Needs (2015)

At the Nexus of Cybersecurity and Public Policy: Some Basic Concepts and Issues (2014)
Emerging and Readily Available Technologies and National Security: A Framework for Addressing Ethical, Legal, and Societal Issues (2014)
Future Directions for NSF Advanced Computing Infrastructure to Support U.S. Science and Engineering in 2017-2020: An Interim Report (2014)
Interim Report of a Review of the Next Generation Air Transportation System Enterprise Architecture, Software, Safety, and Human Factors (2014)

Geotargeted Alerts and Warnings: Report of a Workshop on Current Knowledge and Research Gaps (2013)
Professionalizing the Nation's Cybersecurity Workforce? Criteria for Future Decision-Making (2013)
Public Response to Alerts and Warnings Using Social Media: Summary of a Workshop on Current Knowledge and Research Gaps (2013)

Computing Research for Sustainability (2012)
Continuing Innovation in Information Technology (2012)
The Safety Challenge and Promise of Automotive Electronics: Insights from Unintended Acceleration (2012, with the Board on Energy and Environmental Systems and the Transportation Research Board)

The Future of Computing Performance: Game Over or Next Level? (2011)
Public Response to Alerts and Warnings on Mobile Devices: Summary of a Workshop on Current Knowledge and Research Gaps (2011)
Strategies and Priorities for Information Technology at the Centers for Medicare and Medicaid Services (2011)
Wireless Technology Prospects and Policy Options (2011)

Achieving Effective Acquisition of Information Technology in the Department of Defense (2010)
Critical Code: Software Producibility for Defense (2010)
Improving State Voter Registration Databases (2010)
Proceedings of a Workshop on Deterring Cyberattacks: Informing Strategies and Developing Options for U.S. Policy (2010)
Toward Better Usability, Security, and Privacy of Information Technology: Report of a Workshop (2010)

Limited copies of CSTB reports are available free of charge from

Computer Science and Telecommunications Board
National Academies of Sciences, Engineering, and Medicine
Keck Center of the National Academies
500 Fifth Street, NW, Washington, DC 20001
(202) 334-2605/cstb@nas.edu
www.cstb.org

COMMITTEE FOR A WORKSHOP ON PRIVACY FOR THE INTELLIGENCE COMMUNITY: EMERGING TECHNOLOGIES, ACADEMIC AND INDUSTRY RESEARCH, AND BEST PRACTICES

FRED H. CATE, Indiana University, *Chair*
FREDERICK R. CHANG, Southern Methodist University
TADAYOSHI KOHNO, University of Washington
SUSAN LANDAU, Worcester Polytechnic Institute
HELEN NISSENBAUM, New York University

Staff

EMILY GRUMBLING, Program Officer, Computer Science and Telecommunications Board (CSTB)
JON EISENBERG, Director, CSTB
SHENAE BRADLEY, Administrative Assistant, CSTB
ELIZABETH EULLER, Program Assistant, Board on Energy and Environmental Systems
CHRIS JONES, Financial Manager, Air Force Studies Board

COMPUTER SCIENCE AND TELECOMMUNICATIONS BOARD

FARNAM JAHANIAN, Carnegie Mellon University, *Chair*
LUIZ ANDRÉ BARROSO, Google, Inc.
STEVEN M. BELLOVIN, Columbia University
ROBERT F. BRAMMER, Brammer Technology, LLC
EDWARD FRANK, Brilliant Cloud & Lime Parity
SEYMOUR E. GOODMAN, Georgia Institute of Technology
LAURA HAAS, IBM Corporation
MARK HOROWITZ, Stanford University
MICHAEL KEARNS, University of Pennsylvania
ROBERT KRAUT, Carnegie Mellon University
SUSAN LANDAU, Worcester Polytechnic Institute
PETER LEE, Microsoft Corporation
DAVID E. LIDDLE, US Venture Partners
FRED B. SCHNEIDER, Cornell University
ROBERT F. SPROULL, University of Massachusetts, Amherst
JOHN STANKOVIC, University of Virginia
JOHN A. SWAINSON, Dell, Inc.
ERNEST J. WILSON, University of Southern California
KATHERINE YELICK, University of California, Berkeley

Staff

JON EISENBERG, Director
LYNETTE I. MILLETT, Associate Director

VIRGINIA BACON TALATI, Program Officer
SHENAE BRADLEY, Administrative Assistant
JANEL DEAR, Senior Program Assistant
EMILY GRUMBLING, Program Officer
RENEE HAWKINS, Financial and Administrative Manager
HERBERT S. LIN, Chief Scientist (emeritus)

For more information on CSTB, see its website at http://www.cstb.org, write to CSTB at National Academies of Sciences, Engineering and Medicine, 500 Fifth Street, NW, Washington, DC 20001, call (202) 334-2605, or e-mail the CSTB at cstb@nas.edu.

Acknowledgment of Reviewers

This workshop summary has been reviewed in draft form by individuals chosen for their diverse perspectives and technical expertise, in accordance with procedures approved by the Report Review Committee. The purpose of this independent review is to provide candid and critical comments that will assist the institution in making its published workshop summary as sound as possible and to ensure that the workshop summary meets institutional standards for objectivity, evidence, and responsiveness to the project's charge. The review comments and draft manuscript remain confidential to protect the integrity of the study process. We wish to thank the following individuals for their review of this workshop summary:

Alessandro Acquisti, Carnegie Mellon University,
Fred H. Cate, Indiana University,
Jennifer Glasgow, Acxiom, and
Robert F. Sproull, University of Massachusetts, Amherst.

Although the reviewers listed above have provided many constructive comments and suggestions, they were not asked to endorse the views presented at the workshop, nor did they see the final draft of the workshop summary before its release. The review of this workshop summary was overseen by Samuel H. Fuller, Analog Devices, Inc., who was responsible for making certain that an independent examination of this summary was carried out in accordance with institutional procedures and that all review comments were carefully considered. Responsibility for the final content of this summary rests entirely with the author and the institution.

Contents

1   OVERVIEW   1
    Recurring Themes, 1
        Defining Privacy, 2
        Rapidly Changing Technologies, 2
        Moving Beyond Legal Compliance, 2
        Transparency and Trust, 3
        Organizational Best Practices, 3
        Regulation and Oversight, 4
        Privacy Research Results, Challenges, and Needs, 4
        Individual Preferences and the Privacy Paradox, 5
        Privacy and Society, 6

2   WORKSHOP INTRODUCTION   7
    Welcome, 7
    Background and Context from the Intelligence Community, 7

3   PRIVACY IMPLICATIONS OF EMERGING TECHNOLOGIES PART I—PANEL SUMMARY   9
    Remarks from Panelists, 9
    Panel Discussion, 11
        Emerging Technologies, 11
        User Perceptions and Influence, 12
    Open Discussion, 13

4   PRIVACY IMPLICATIONS OF EMERGING TECHNOLOGIES PART II—PANEL SUMMARY   14
    Remarks from Panelists, 14
    Panel Discussion, 16
        Unintended Consequences of Data Collection and Use, 16
        Emerging Technologies with Potential Consequences, 16
        The Evolution of Multiparty Interaction with Data, 17
        Collection of Data about One User that Reveals Information about Someone Else, 17
        Industry Practice as a Potential for the IC, 18
        Defining Privacy, 18
    Open Discussion, 19
        Challenges Around Control and Use Frameworks, 19
        Best Technical Practices, 19

5   SOCIAL SCIENCE AND BEHAVIORAL ECONOMICS OF PRIVACY—PANEL SUMMARY   21
    Remarks from Panelists, 21
    Panel Discussion, 24
        Recent Examples of Tipping Points, 24
        Anticipating Future Tipping Points, 25

        Improving Trust, 25
    Open Discussion, 27
        Public Perceptions and Trust, 27
        Equality, Discrimination, and Consumer Profiling, 28
        Privacy Research, 29

6 BEST PRACTICES AND ETHICAL APPROACHES FOR DATA COLLECTION AND USE—PANEL SUMMARY   31
    Remarks from Panelists, 31
    Panel Discussion, 34
    Open Discussion, 35
        Regulations and Internal Standards, 35
        Privacy in the Context of Organizational Missions, 36
        Transparency, Oversight, and Trust, 36

7 WRAP-UP—PANEL SUMMARY   39
    Closing, 41

APPENDIXES

A	Workshop Statement of Task	45
B	Workshop Agenda	46
C	Biographical Sketches	48
D	Acronyms and Abbreviations	56

1

Overview

The Computer Science and Telecommunications Board (CSTB) convened a workshop on July 21-22, 2015, to advance dialogues on privacy between technical and policy staff of the Intelligence Community (IC) and outside experts from academia and the private sector. CSTB is a standing board of the National Academies of Sciences, Engineering, and Medicine. The workshop was sponsored by the Office of the Director of National Intelligence (ODNI).

To conduct this workshop, a workshop steering committee was appointed to identify potential speakers and design the workshop agenda. The committee and Academies staff worked with ODNI to invite staff from IC agencies. Approximately 40 participants, including the steering committee, invited panelists, IC staff and officials, and Academies staff, participated in the 1½-day workshop held in Washington, D.C.

This report has been prepared by the workshop rapporteur as a factual summary of what occurred at the workshop. The steering committee's role was limited to planning and convening the workshop. The views contained in the report are those of individual workshop participants and do not necessarily represent the views of their employers, the workshop participants as a whole, the steering committee, the Academies, the sponsor, or any other affiliated organizations.

The workshop was designed around the following three major areas:

1. Privacy implications of emerging technologies,
2. Public and individual preferences and attitudes toward privacy and the social science and behavioral economics of privacy, and
3. Ethical approaches to data collection and use.

Two panels were devoted to the first topic, one panel was devoted to the second and one to the third.

The workshop was designed to be as interactive as possible, with an emphasis on discussion and engagement rather than lengthy presentations. Opening remarks were delivered by Fred H. Cate, workshop steering committee chair and C. Ben Dutton Professor of Law at Indiana University, and Alexander W. Joel, civil liberties protection officer, ODNI. Each panel was moderated by a member of the steering committee, with the following format: panelists each presented 5 minutes of opening remarks, participated in a moderated panel discussion, and then engaged in open discussion with all workshop participants. The workshop concluded with a final wrap-up panel, during which participants summarized and discussed key points and reflections from the proceedings.

RECURRING THEMES

Workshop discussions focused on privacy implications of various technologies and practices, individual privacy preferences and behaviors, privacy policies and practices of organizations, and the broader societal impacts of privacy. In particular, the invited speakers from academia and the private sector each provided his or her expertise and/or perspectives, with content ranging from academic research on consumer privacy behaviors to corporate strategies for privacy assessment; lessons from academia and the private sector were often discussed in the context of the work of the IC.

Several themes recurred throughout the workshop. To assist the reader, recurring themes are briefly discussed below.

Defining Privacy

Many participants noted that "privacy" means different things to different people, and that this can vary highly with context. It was suggested that the term is often used to connote a range of associated values or principles; throughout the workshop, a range of examples emerged, such as trust, security, the right to be forgotten, freedom, and anonymity.

One panelist identified a common definition of privacy as "the ability to control what happens to one's information." Others defined privacy violations, or issues, in terms of whether a given practice, policy, or action regarding personal information might be perceived as negative by a stakeholder (for example, individuals or regulators).

Participants discussed different conceptions of privacy, touching on both legal and philosophical considerations. Several participants suggested that it may not be possible or practical to develop a universal definition of privacy largely due to its contextual nature. Someone suggested that the inability to be defined is an intrinsic characteristic of privacy, and that it is something that society must struggle over. A panelist pointed out that an inability to clearly define or quantify privacy could confound those working toward protecting it. Another participant suggested that privacy might be easier to understand and address by focusing on one of its associated values or principles at a time.

Rapidly Changing Technologies

Two of the panels focused on the privacy implications of emerging technologies, touching on the Internet of Things, smart and connected vehicles, mobile communications and devices, biometrics, health information technology (IT), cloud/edge computing, big data analytics (data mining, aggregation, etc.), and online advertising. It was noted that computing technologies have become ubiquitous, and that there are more and more ways and places that data are being collected.

One of the panelists noted a shift in some emerging technologies from privacy by trust (where individuals must have faith that technology services will not misuse their data) to privacy by design (where privacy is considered during every phase of the design process to minimize potential privacy issues), citing the evolution of approaches to smart and connected vehicles.

In general, participants noted that privacy implications of emerging technologies can be hard to anticipate. In particular, a panelist pointed out that transformative technologies are often fundamentally new, so it can be hard to predict how they will be used and what privacy implications could emerge. One of the panelists described a tool developed in her research group to help software developers identify potential privacy and fairness issues in their code.

Moving Beyond Legal Compliance

Multiple participants suggested that organizational compliance with existing laws and regulations around data practices is not sufficient to protect privacy and/or preserve public trust in an organization that works with potentially sensitive data. Laws and regulations take time to create, so they often lag behind technological advances. Several participants suggested that the fact that a practice or action is not illegal does not make it acceptable; privacy is defined by values, not the laws that aim to uphold them, and people have reacted negatively to perceived as well as actual privacy violations. Multiple participants suggested that organizations must develop and continuously adapt their own internal policies and practices to protect privacy—beyond those that are legally mandated—in order to be effective and maintain the trust of their stakeholders and the public. A participant suggested that the public wants to see evidence that their data are treated with care and respect.

Transparency and Trust

Many workshop participants suggested that transparency is critical for building trust in an organization or a technology. Several panelists suggested that individuals may be more likely to trust a given tool or service if they are (1) provided contextual information on how it works and how it uses individuals' data, or (2) given more control over this use.

It was also pointed out that, due to the generally secret nature of its mission, the IC likely does not have access to the same transparency-enabling tools or mechanisms available to private sector organizations. Several participants noted that transparency does not necessarily require direct disclosure of an organization's practices or the specific data that it is using. For example, an organization could provide illustrative rather than actual examples of its practices, or it could provide transparency to a trusted third-party or oversight body, who might then provide assurance to the public that a given practice is considered and appropriate.

There was also discussion about how public perception impacts trust. A participant pointed out that transparency about a given practice can generate trust, and make individuals more likely to give an organization the benefit of the doubt in future cases.

Several participants implied that trust can be justified or misplaced, and productive or undermining to privacy. At least one participant raised the issue of "pseudo-transparency," when individuals falsely believe (or are led to believe) that they have an accurate understanding of (and/or control over) how their data are being used, which could lead to misguided trust and complacency. Another participant suggested that publicity about pseudo-transparency could potentially lead to public outcry.

Multiple participants suggested that building trust is not simple, and that it takes time. Many suggested that an organization can build trust by being more transparent—for example, about how data are used and the value they generate (to consumers or society), steps taken to protect privacy, and oversight mechanisms. Several participants suggested that building trust requires a long-term commitment to clear and accurate communication, both within an organization and externally.

Organizational Best Practices

There was much discussion about strategies that organizations have taken, or might take, to protect privacy and improve trust. Several participants from the private sector noted that it can take time for an organization to develop the rigorous data management practices needed to protect privacy and build trust with users or constituents. They suggested that the process is iterative, and that an organization's practices can develop and improve with time through sustained effort, evaluation, engagement with stakeholders, and adjustment. Multiple participants pointed out various factors, such as changes in technological capabilities, legal requirements, or individuals' privacy expectations, that make it difficult to anticipate potential privacy challenges or concerns. Several participants suggested that privacy is a moving target, and that an organization must be willing to continuously revisit, evaluate, and adapt its practices to best accommodate the changing privacy landscape.

There was some discussion of how organizations might operationalize privacy decision-making. Several participants discussed the strategy of asking whether revealing a given data practice would embarrass the organization. Several participants from the private sector noted the contextual nature of privacy and suggested that each decision must be evaluated individually, with consideration for all stakeholder impacts.

There was some discussion of important roles within an organization. For example, individuals can be designated to promote privacy as a core value beyond simple legal compliance, propose alternative strategies, and anticipate future challenges. Organizations can establish internal mechanisms for privacy oversight. Several participants pointed out that some organizations have limited resources; a panelist suggested that a small core group of privacy professionals might be augmented by designating one or more people within each operational unit as privacy liaisons to the core.

Regulation and Oversight

There was some discussion of internal vs. external regulation and oversight of government and private sector organizations' data privacy practices. Several participants suggested that internal regulation could be more responsive, agile, and thorough than external regulation. Another participant suggested that external regulations might prompt organizations to focus on compliance rather than outcomes, and also might lag behind current technologies. Others suggested that internal regulation is subject to bias toward an organization's own interest, and that external regulation is necessary for transparency. Many participants noted that external input, guidance, or oversight could help to bring balance, and to build trust among those external stakeholders whose privacy is at stake.

Privacy Research Results, Challenges, and Needs

One of the functions of the workshop was to expose members of the IC to outside research related to privacy. Multiple panelists discussed their own research, as described below.

- Fuming Shih, senior product manager, Oracle Cloud, discussed his research around smart phone user privacy preferences and behaviors.
- Steven M. Bellovin, Percy K. and Vidal L. W. Hudson Professor of Computer Science, Columbia University, noted that his research involves creating a new formal definition of privacy and the harms that result from various activities.
- Carl Gunter, professor of computer science, University of Illinois, provided insights from his work on privacy and security in health IT.
- Roxana Geambasu, assistant professor of computer science, Columbia University, discussed her research aimed at increasing privacy online, including the development of tools to help users understand how their personal data are tracked and used, and to help programmers detect "privacy bugs" while developing applications.
- Idris Adjerid, assistant professor of management, University of Notre Dame, discussed his research on the economics of privacy with a focus on behavioral economics.
- Jessica Staddon, associate professor of computer science, North Carolina State University, discussed some of her work related to user perceptions of transparency tools.
- Joseph Turow, Robert Lewis Shayon Professor of Communication at the Annenberg School for Communication, University of Pennsylvania, discussed his survey research related to digital relationships and surveillance in the context of marketing and retailing, including results of a recent survey addressing consumer attitudes about private sector tracking and collection of their data.

Workshop discussions also addressed the broader privacy research landscape, and multiple participants highlighted challenges associated with work in this area. Several suggested that massive private sector data sets are generally underutilized for research purposes, probably because of disincentives for such research in the private sector. One participant suggested that academic researchers tend to be limited to small data sets and generally lack access to private-sector data.

Several participants suggested that some studies on privacy preferences and behaviors have yielded conflicting results. It was pointed out that surveys and studies must be carefully designed, and results and individual behaviors carefully interpreted, in order to yield meaningful conclusions. A participant identified the need for a culture of repeatability, and for consistency and objectivity in measurement. Several participants noted existing strategies for such design and interpretation of experiments and surveys, and reiterated the highly contextual nature of privacy.

Several participants called attention to areas in which little research has been done and where more would be helpful, including the following:

- How individuals feel about their own privacy vs. that of others,
- Whether secrecy undermines trust,
- Privacy preferences among different demographic groups, such as lower-income populations and minority groups, and
- Social (rather than individual) costs and benefits of privacy.

Several participants discussed the notion of a "science of privacy." A member of the workshop steering committee suggested that, within this framework, grand challenge problems could be identified and data sets could be developed and shared to advance privacy research. Another pondered whether such a formal framework might help organizations develop tools for operationalizing privacy decision-making. One participant suggested that the contextual nature of privacy could make this very difficult, and another pointed out that the field of ethics already offers a rigorous basis for deriving actionable principles. Many suggested that more research about privacy is needed.

A member of the workshop steering committee suggested that researchers might be able to make progress on some of the IC's privacy challenges if given "toy problems," or representative problems, that can be shared publicly but embody critical challenges. Another member suggested that deeper engagement between the IC and academia could facilitate stronger communication of the IC's commitment to compliance around privacy.

Individual Preferences and the Privacy Paradox

Several participants pointed out the phenomenon of individuals who say they care about privacy but nonetheless seemingly act against their own interest, termed by one as the "privacy paradox." Possible reasons for such behavior were discussed. In particular, several participants suggested that individuals often do not have the time or knowledge to deduce the privacy implications of their actions or to learn what they may do to enhance privacy. They also may not understand how a given technology works, or what companies are doing with their data. A panelist noted that humans do not always behave rationally in the economic sense, especially when it comes to privacy decisions. It was also suggested that there may be tension between what an individual believes to be "the right thing," and what he or she wants in the moment. Another panelist suggested that an individual's intuition or level of familiarity with a given app or service might play a large role in individual decision-making.

Several participants cautioned against the common assumption that people are comfortable giving up their data in exchange for the benefits of using a given technology or service, suggesting that this is a faulty assumption. One panelist suggested that fair trade-offs between privacy and utility are not feasible, due to the limited number of options provided for how to use a technology or a service, and because the value of an individual's data depends upon what other data exist that they might be combined with and how, and is thus always changing and difficult to pin down. The panelist also suggested that, for these reasons, any notion of a "privacy market" will fail. Another panelist noted survey evidence suggesting that many individuals actually feel resigned to the fact that their data are being collected, and feel that this condition is simply beyond their control. Several participants suggested that consumers may feel that the use of various technologies, such as the Internet or mobile devices, is an all-or-nothing proposition: Either they get the convenience of these technologies while giving away data they would actually prefer not to share, or simply do not get to use the technology.

There was also some discussion of the idea of "tipping points," that is, points at which individuals' perspectives on a technology or practice shift, causing them to alter their behavior or attitudes, possibly by ceasing to use a given tool or by pushing back against a given practice. A participant suggested that tipping points likely occur at the individual rather than societal level, but that a series of mini-events that trigger tipping points could cause a critical mass of individuals to change their perspectives. There was some discussion of visible events that might fall into this category, such as the abuses investigated by the Church committee, the Office of Personnel Management (OPM) breach, the Ashley Madison breach, and the Snowden disclosures.

Privacy and Society

Many participants noted societal benefits of data collection and use, for example, to advance public health or national security. One participant suggested that the field of health IT could be a valuable evolving case study on balancing the use of information for public good (such as disease prevention) with individual privacy.

Several participants suggested that while privacy is often considered an individual value, privacy itself can also have important, collective societal benefits that are not always taken into account. For example, private and anonymous voting can help promote robust democracy, and privacy can empower individuals to explore non-majoritarian views and facilitate freedom of thought.

Several participants also suggested that certain demographic groups may be disproportionately impacted by privacy issues, and that such impacts may be undercounted. It was also pointed out that little research has been done on how privacy preferences vary between demographic groups. Several participants suggested that more research is needed in these areas.

Several participants noted that recent discussions around big data and privacy have emphasized protection of privacy via control of how data are used rather than by limiting their collection. One participant suggested that privacy advocates are uncomfortable with this notion, because even the best use control policies can be changed in ways that open up pathways for unintended or harmful use of stored data: If data do not exist, none can be abused. Another participant pointed out that the public seems to have accepted the practice of massive collection and aggregation of data even in the absence of a rigorous argument demonstrating that this is defensible, and suggested that there might be value in revisiting this acceptance.

There was also some discussion about evolving societal values. One participant suggested that the principles underlying existing societal norms were honed over time from important societal values, and they should not simply be discarded as technology advances. A participant questioned whether these underlying values were being upended by the rapid evolution of technology. Several participants cautioned against the notion that technology itself is an uncontrollable force, and suggested that we should focus not only on emerging technologies, but also on how they are deployed throughout society.

2

Workshop Introduction

WELCOME

Fred H. Cate, chair of the workshop steering committee, opened the meeting by summarizing the goals and structure of the workshop. He noted that the workshop was organized by the National Academies of Sciences, Engineering, and Medicine and sponsored by ODNI in order to help advance dialogue between members of the IC and outside experts and practitioners around the topic of privacy.

Specifically, the workshop was designed to address (1) privacy challenges presented by new technologies, (2) ways of understanding the public's behavior and attitudes about data collection and use, and (3) methodologies for making decisions about data collection and use that go beyond mere compliance with the law. A particular goal of the workshop was to address challenges that might impinge on trust around personal privacy, and strategies for anticipating or managing these challenges in ways that might enhance trust.

BACKGROUND AND CONTEXT FROM THE INTELLIGENCE COMMUNITY

Alexander W. Joel, civil liberties protection officer, Office of the Director of National Intelligence, noted that the group had convened to help improve understanding of how to protect the security and privacy of U.S. citizens and people around the world. He pointed out that 2015 was the 40th anniversary of the Church committee,[1] whose examination of past abuses in the intelligence arena led to major reforms. He noted that the committee did conclude that certain intelligence activities serve proper and necessary ends of the government, and should be preserved under effective restraints. He suggested that the IC's current governance framework is largely defined by the changes made in response to the Church committee's 1976 report, including the establishment of congressional oversight committees and strengthened legal oversight within the executive branch. He added that the Foreign Intelligence Surveillance Act (FISA) court currently provides oversight from the judicial branch as well.

Joel noted that, while much has since changed in the world, members of the IC still believe that the existing rules and governance framework provide effective guidance on maintaining balance between security and privacy. He noted that some in the public clearly disagree, and that this divergence of views was part of what the workshop was convened to address.

He read a quote from President Obama:

---

[1] The United States Senate Select Committee to Study Governmental Operations with Respect to Intelligence Activities, chaired by Senator Frank Church, was formed in 1975 in response to "great public concern that the Congress take action to bring the intelligence agencies under the constitutional framework," according to Senator Church's letter of transmittal. The committee's report was released in April 1976 (Select Committee to Study Governmental Operations with Respect to Intelligence Activities, 1976, *Intelligence Activities and the Rights of Americans Book II: Final Report of the United States Senate Select Committee to Study Governmental Operations with Respect to Intelligence Activities*, Washington, D.C.: U.S. Government Printing Office).

Those who are troubled by our existing programs are not interested in repeating the tragedy of 9/11, and those who defend these programs are not dismissive of civil liberties. The challenge is getting the details right, and that is not simple.[2]

He pointed out that the rapid pace of technological change makes the challenge more difficult, but that technology concerns are not new. He quoted Justice Brandeis's famous 1928 dissent in *Olmstead v. United States*:[3]

The progress of science in furnishing the Government with means of espionage is not likely to stop with wire-tapping. Ways may someday be developed by which the Government, without removing papers from secret drawers, can reproduce them in court, and by which it will be enabled to expose to a jury the most intimate occurrences of the home.[4]

A similar caution appeared in the Church committee's report:

In an era where the technological capability of government relentlessly increases, we must be wary of the drift toward "big brother government." The potential for abuse is awesome and requires special attention to fashioning restraints, which not only cure past problems, but anticipate and prevent the future misuse of technology.[5]

Joel observed that people often focus on current problems, rather than thinking ahead. He then discussed some of the policy challenges associated with technological change. Many current policies or rules were put into place years ago—even centuries ago, in the case of the United States Constitution. He suggested that this does not mean such rules are bad, but just that we need to figure out how best to apply them.

He suggested that rules and policies tailored to current technologies are unlikely to succeed; policy makers are not experts in technology, and the policy process is relatively slow compared to the pace of technology change. How society should manage the inevitable gap between the rules in place and current technological practices is an open question.

Joel noted that insights into how people value privacy in different contexts would help to enhance understanding of privacy implications of different technologies. Discussion of ethics and best practices in the private sector and elsewhere in the government for big data collection, use, and analysis, would help inform the IC and others about how to fashion responses to emerging privacy challenges.

Joel also discussed the value of transparency and of dialog both between the IC and the public, and between members of the technology and policy communities in advancing dialogues and making progress on privacy. He noted that more transparency will enable the IC to better inform and explain its role to the public, including the rules it obeys and how, and the nature of and need for its activities. He also suggested that technologists and policy experts often share the same goals, whether or not they always speak the same language.

---

[2] Executive Office of the President, "Remarks by the President on Review of Signals Intelligence," January 17, 2014, https://www.whitehouse.gov/the-press-office/2014/01/17/remarks-president-review-signals-intelligence.

[3] *Olmstead v. United States*, 277 U.S. 438 (1928).

[4] Mr. Joel noted that, while it may sound as if Justice Brandeis was predicting the cloud, he was actually talking about developments in the psychic sciences—a fact about this opinion that is not commonly discussed.

[5] Select Committee to Study Governmental Operations with Respect to Intelligence Activities, 1976, *Intelligence Activities and the Rights of Americans Book II: Final Report of the United States Senate Select Committee to Study Governmental Operations with Respect to Intelligence Activities*, Washington, D.C.: U.S. Government Printing Office, p. 289.

3

Privacy Implications of Emerging Technologies Part I—Panel Summary

REMARKS FROM PANELISTS

Susan Landau, panel moderator and professor of cybersecurity policy at Worcester Polytechnic Institute, launched the session by observing that views around the privacy significance of metadata have changed in the past few years; people have become more aware that metadata can actually enable the extraction of sensitive information. She provided an example, noting that Google captures information about how users swipe their Android phones. Analysis of this metadata can inform improvements to the product's design, but it could also be used to infer mood.

She observed that the many potential privacy implications of metadata illustrate the challenges posed by emerging technologies. Landau, as moderator, then introduced the following panelists and gave each of them 5 minutes for opening comments:

- Fuming Shih, senior product manager, Oracle Cloud;
- Tao Zhang, distinguished engineer, Cisco Systems;
- Mark McGovern, CEO, Mobile System 7; and,
- Lee Tien, senior staff attorney and Adams Chair for Internet Rights, Electronic Frontier Foundation.

Fuming Shih presented some results from his research on user privacy preferences and behaviors with smart phones, including the factors that affect individual preferences for information disclosure to mobile apps, and on ways of making privacy conflicts more visible to users.

Shih introduced the concept of privacy "tipping points"—individual user experiences or thresholds that precipitate a shift in thinking about a given technology and can alter user privacy preferences and behaviors. He cited his own experience with the Google Now feature on an Android smart phone, in which the phone notified him, unprompted, that it was time to head home for the day, having "learned" his commuting habits by tracking his past behaviors. This experience caused him to rethink the amount of data he was comfortable sharing.

Shih then summarized several useful themes from his research findings about individuals' behaviors around privacy.

1. *Context matters*. The details of a given circumstance are critical to understanding why people disclose—or do not disclose—their information.
2. *Trust matters more*. Shih's research findings suggest that trust outweighs context in individual decision-making. People often rely on their intuitive trust in a device or app when deciding whether to share their information. He also found that a user's level of familiarity with an app influenced data-sharing decisions more than the content of the app's privacy policy, suggesting that improvements to privacy policies may not have much effect. Shih also suggested that revealing more information on the context of data use may make users feel like they have more control and make them more willing to trust an app or device.

3. *Privacy is complicated.* Shih found that reasons for disclosing—or not disclosing—information vary between individuals. He suggested that understanding *why* people disclose is more important than *what* people disclose.

Tao Zhang started by noting that there are currently approximately 12 billion networked "things" worldwide. Analysis by Cisco and others suggests that there will be more than 50 billion devices connected to the Internet by 2020, in industrial systems, manufacturing plants, public services, connected vehicles, and consumer devices. There is even interest in embedding passive or active communication devices into people's clothing.

Zhang expects that the world will become connected beyond what many of us can imagine today. This means that whenever we (or our devices) communicate, we will leave traces of ourselves behind—whether knowingly or unknowingly. Information will be left in many places, providing new opportunities for collection, and making it more difficult to enforce data collection and use policies.

He noted that people are becoming increasingly aware of the privacy implications of these technologies; they want to do something about it, but run into the challenge of competing requirements. For example, privacy and security can sometimes conflict; providing privacy on a network means hiding a user's identity—or concealing his traces—which enables malicious actors to hide as well.

Mark McGovern began by making an analogy between security and privacy, noting that both can be difficult to define, and can mean different things to different stakeholders. He went on to discuss potential privacy implications of security technologies. In particular, enterprises are increasingly relying on mobile devices and storing data in the cloud. The increased number of access points creates uncertainty about who is using systems, increasing the need to monitor user activity. This trend could have the effect of tracking authorized users in a way they would not appreciate.

McGovern described the importance of balancing the needs of customers, investors, analysts, and team members when taking steps to improve security; security tools are often built before rules of acceptable practice have been established, necessitating a proactive approach to product support and build-out based upon the needs of investors, customers, users, and the public. He suggested that similar considerations likely apply to privacy as well.

Lee Tien addressed three main points: (1) the nature of privacy, (2) privacy as a social product, and (3) trust and transparency.

First, he identified privacy as an "essentially contested topic,"[1] and suggested that it—not unlike beauty or justice—is not truly capable of being defined. He suggested that it is in fact a constitutive feature of privacy that its meaning must be debated over and developed by society—it cannot simply be prescribed by a determined formula. He pointed out that the Constitution does not say much about privacy, though it is appealed to in the First and Fourth Amendments, consistent with this picture.

He suggested that there are many different conceptions of privacy. Within the legal field, conceptions relate to the First, Fourth, and Fifth Amendments, associational privacy, and decisions in cases such as *National Association for the Advancement of Colored People v. Alabama*. Tien stated that all of these ideas are relevant to privacy discussions both within and outside the IC, but pointed out that people have many different worldviews and perspectives.

Tien then identified the notion of privacy as a social product, referencing the ideas of sociologists such as Howard Becker and Erving Goffman. He suggested that privacy is something that people create over time, based upon experiences, with the resources available. For example, an individual may create privacy by putting a letter into an envelope, or by going into a phone booth and closing the door. He identified encryption as a contemporary resource for the social production of privacy in a computerized world. He suggested that

---

[1] W. Bryce Gallie, 1955, Essentially contested concepts, *Proceedings of the Aristotelian Society*, High Wycombe, U.K.: Harrison & Sons.

the use of a resource is necessary: Without the ability to mark a boundary, it is hard to achieve or demonstrate an expectation of privacy.

Tien echoed the sentiment that transparency is essential to any meaningful trust relationship, and suggested that transparency is important both before and after a privacy incident. He pointed out that a lack of knowledge at both the individual and societal levels makes it difficult for individuals to assess privacy impacts. For example, consumers often believe that the existence of a privacy policy means that their data are being protected against use by third parties, which is a false notion. He suggested that public knowledge of data practices is necessary for assessing and creating privacy.

PANEL DISCUSSION

Landau led the panel in discussion of privacy implications of some emerging technologies, as summarized below.

Emerging Technologies

Landau asked the panelists to comment on the privacy implications of technologies such as the Internet of Things, mobile devices, and notifications.

McGovern pointed out that emerging technologies such as the Internet of Things are changing rapidly. As consumers and developers learn more about these technologies, their privacy expectations will change. The significant lag between the development and adoption of new technologies poses a large risk that developers will fail to anticipate privacy implications and user expectations around these technologies.

Zhang noted that concern has risen around the potential for correlating data collected from different streams (as in the Internet of Things) to identify information about a given user. Such concerns generally prompted users to want more control over their data, and have helped spur development of enhanced user control mechanisms, such as user options for encryption and data storage schemes.

Shih questioned whether enhanced user control options would actually enhance privacy. He pointed out that some smart phones have hundreds of permissions or control options, resulting in a complex and poorly understood set of options. In his work on the Android system, he found that privacy choices are also often presented at bad times. For example, users are unlikely to read the permissions requirements carefully after downloading an app that they want to use immediately. Tien added that many people are truly surprised to learn how much can be inferred about an individual's intimate details by analyzing seemingly innocuous data about their online purchases and other activities. He noted a huge gap between the technologically literate and the general public in their level of understanding of privacy risks, and that many have been surprised to learn of this gap, even in the corporate world.

According to Zhang, over the past 20 years, computing has shifted from local processing to the cloud, and most recently to "edge" models, which combine local and cloud computing and storage to minimize latency and increase performance. This has resulted in more distributed computing and storage, which can have additional privacy impacts. In particular, the increase in local storage minimizes the amount of data that are shared, but also means that personal information must be protected in more locations.

McGovern addressed notifications, suggesting that they can expose some of the less-visible functions of connected objects and devices. Unexpected notifications can make people realize that systems have learned something about them. Tien distinguished between notifications generated on a given device using locally stored data and notifications generated based upon data from somewhere on the cloud. While the privacy implications in each case are different, users may not be able to tell the difference. Shih described results suggesting that notifications about data collection may prompt a portion of users to opt out of a service entirely, but otherwise have minimal impact on most users' behavior.

Zhang noted several emerging privacy concerns about connected vehicles. The navigation systems may store data in the vehicle that could be related to driving habits, and potentially be correlated with geolocation, time, and other information. The vehicles' networks provide potential pathways for accessing these data. He pointed out that there has been much debate about ownership of this sort of data. Some say that all of a vehicle's data should be considered private, but others note that much of the collected data would enable car companies to improve vehicle function and maintenance. This is an open question, but much user data have been collected already.

Tien pointed out some emerging policy challenges with respect to connected vehicles. For example, some in California have proposed replacing the gas tax with a mileage-based tax that could potentially be determined either by tracking vehicle location over time or, alternatively, via some data-free method. He noted that perspectives about geolocation data have evolved over the past 7 years or so, owing partly to empirical studies showing how easy it can be to identify individuals based upon their physical paths. In this context, courts have found a reasonable expectation of privacy under the Fourth Amendment, in contrast to past decisions finding that individuals do not have a reasonable expectation of privacy if they are visible on a public road. Such shifts underscore the challenge of determining what counts as private.

User Perceptions and Influence

Zhang explained that privacy has traditionally been generally supported by trust—we expect that data collectors will not abuse the information they hold. However, the public does not always consider this sufficient. The general idea of "privacy by design," where privacy is considered at all phases of the engineering process, is becoming more common in certain contexts.[2] For example, he suggested that customer concerns have been the major driver of joint work between industry and the Department of Transportation on designing privacy-preserving security systems for cars. Specifically, collision avoidance systems will require communication among a critical mass of vehicles to be effective, making it likely that such connectivity will be mandated in the future, prompting privacy concerns. Efforts are now under way to build communications systems that will not exchange data that could enable tracking of individual vehicles.

Shih suggested that most phone users seem to have the false notion that their data is not really at risk—for example, thinking that only celebrities will have their photos stolen and leaked. He suggested that people who do have concerns have no direct channel to voice them to phone designers.

Zhang suggested that the magnitude of users' reactions to privacy issues depends on both the perceived value of a given product and the perceived user control over its functions. For example, the value of products such as smart phones is perceived to be high relative to the potential risk of information leaks; however, if significant risks become visible, or if users perceive that they do not really have choices, a tipping point can occur. Users may or may not provide feedback when they have privacy concerns, but often simply abandon a product. Shih added that his research suggests that both the accurate perception of control and the illusion of control make users more willing to stick with a product or situation.

Tien pointed out that receipt of customer concerns can prompt companies to simply reduce the visibility of the problematic functions, and postponing these solutions can result in much larger problems down the road. McGovern pointed out that future complications also arise due to the ambition of technology developers; indeed, it can be difficult to anticipate the societal impacts of audacious technologies. He also suggested that regulated industries are very aware of privacy issues, and are often more sophisticated in their questions about the risk of storing privacy-sensitive information. He suggested that other sectors, such as manufacturing, pharmaceuticals, and biotech, may be more focused on security than on end-user privacy. Tien added that there are many companies, such as data brokers, whose customers are not the individual end users, so individuals' interests or privacy concerns may not be very visible to them. However, widely held public perceptions and bad publicity can create some push-back. Attention from legislators can also move companies to make privacy improvements.

---

[2] For background on this concept, see A. Cavoukian, 2009, "Privacy by Design: The 7 Foundational Principles," Information and Privacy Commissioner of Ontario, Canada, https://www.ipc.on.ca/english/Privacy /Introduction-to-PbD/.

The panel also touched on the siloing of data as a technical control, challenges with verification of such controls, and the complement and interplay between legal and technical controls in providing accountability.

OPEN DISCUSSION

A participant cautioned against accepting the notion that users are willing to give up privacy in exchange for value. One of the panelists pointed out that true trade-offs may not even be possible because there is not a sufficient range of choices to enable a fair trade.

The group further discussed notions of trust. A panelist suggested that organizations earn trust not just by following the rules at hand, but by also acting with consideration and restraint. Another panelist suggested that people care most about privacy only after something bad has happened, and that explaining what happened and demonstrating how the problems are being addressed could help to strengthen trust. Other participants pointed out that a user's trust in a technology may reflect an accurate understanding of a technology's protections, but it could also reflect positive past experiences with a technology, ignorance about its underlying functions, or resignation to a lack of other options. In that sense, trust can be positive or negative, justified or misplaced, and productive or undermining to privacy.

The group went on to discuss smart vehicles. One participant noted that vehicles already contain dozens of computers and collect a significant and increasing amount of data. Another also noted that the general public may not understand the implications or details of this or future collection, even if notice of such collection is given.

Some participants commented on incentives in the private sector. One participant pointed out that a firm may have an incentive to maximize its ability to collect data while alleviating customer concern by providing superficial elements of control and notice. Another participant noted that the potential for individuals to be satisfied with superficial controls is a serious concern. One of the panelists noted that companies are focused on their business goals (often with good intentions), and that their attention to privacy will similarly be driven by economics. Greater attention to privacy might be encouraged by a reduction in the cost of doing the right thing, the presence of regulatory oversight, or increasing the value of privacy-respecting products. Another participant suggested that services and businesses whose competitiveness is tied strongly to their reputations are likely to be more attuned to privacy, and suggested that the companies have more technological capacity and expertise than their governance organizations.

It was noted by a participant that the IC does not have at its disposal the same tools that companies have for building trust with individuals, such as notifications and the "right to tinker" with technologies, and has had varying success in communicating either its privacy-protecting measures or the benefits the public derives from intelligence activities. The participant asked how the IC might best approach the question of trust with the public.

A panelist agreed that the IC and law enforcement have a limited set of tools for building trust; for example, individual notification of the subject of an investigation is not an option, except after the fact. He suggested that one might consider the proxies for the citizen in different contexts, for example the Congress, and work with them on enhancing disclosure and transparency. But he also suggested that the congressional oversight process itself may need reevaluation. Another panelist suggested that trust could be gained by providing representative or model examples of how data are used, so that the public can understand the safeguards that are in place today, the privacy impact of different practices, and how those practices contribute to the public good. One of the panelists added that the government and the private sector play different roles in society, and one should not expect practices that are acceptable in the private sector to also be acceptable in the government sector.

Finally, a panelist asked how society characterizes "sufficient privacy." He suggested that, without an answer, it will be hard to know whether we are on the right path.

4

Privacy Implications of Emerging Technologies Part II—Panel Summary

REMARKS FROM PANELISTS

Tadayoshi Kohno, the Short-Dooley Professor of Computer Science and Engineering at the University of Washington, began the session by noting that the next panel would also focus on emerging technologies, with an emphasis on analytics and the cloud. He encouraged the participants to prepare questions to pose to panelists during the open discussion session. Kohno, as moderator, then introduced the following panelists and gave each of them 5 minutes for opening comments:

- Carl Gunter, professor of computer science, University of Illinois;
- Roxana Geambasu, assistant professor of computer science, Columbia University;
- Steven M. Bellovin, Percy K. and Vidal L. W. Hudson Professor of Computer Science, Columbia University; and,
- James L. Wayman, research administrator, San Jose State University.

Carl Gunter discussed privacy implications of the growing use and collection of digital health data. He distinguished between "health care" technologies (tools for diagnosis and treatment of disease) and "health" technologies (the quickly growing market of tools for disease prevention and encouragement of healthy habits, such as the Fitbit), and suggested that these two areas may be moving toward a disruptive convergence.

Gunter described emerging capabilities in analysis of both structured and semi-structured data, including doctor's notes or even information from a Fitbit or an Apple watch, and noted that data mining of electronic health records (EHRs) has led to the identification of prescription drug risks. Such capabilities could have enormous societal benefits, but they require access to large quantities of data about individuals, who may not want their records to be accessible even for such purposes.

He suggested that the rapidly changing field of health IT has a number of characteristics that could make it a useful laboratory for monitoring privacy trends and developments, including the following:

- There are many stakeholders with competing interests;
- Regulations and rules are evolving;
- Privacy provisions in existing laws such as the Health Insurance Portability and Accountability Act (HIPAA) and the Health Information Technology for Economic and Clinical Health (HITECH) Act were developed following much public debate and negotiation;
- The field is seeing increased use of distributed networks where institutions hold data to support research, but share answers to research queries on their data;
- Analysis of health data can yield great public benefit (in the form of medical breakthroughs and advances in public health); and
- Collection and analysis of data can pose privacy risks.

In particular, the field could be a valuable, evolving case study on balancing the use of information for public good with individual rights to privacy.

Roxana Geambasu discussed her research on increasing privacy online. Her work emphasizes enabling development and design with privacy in mind, and increasing user awareness of the privacy implications of their online actions.

She noted that privacy is scarce on the Internet; indeed, many users are eager to share their data online and many services aggressively collect and use that information. Today's Web services collect immense amounts of information, including every click and every site we visit, and mine our documents and emails. This data can be used to target ads or fine-tune prices, sometimes to the benefit of the user and sometimes not. Users are generally unaware of how such data are used or abused by the collectors.

Geambasu described XRay, a tool developed by her research group that can reveal how Web services use personal data for targeting or personalization. It works by monitoring user inputs and outputs from these services, and identifies correlations using test accounts populated with subsets of a user's information. She noted that the tool has proved remarkably accurate (around 80-90 percent precision) with Gmail, YouTube, and Amazon. By increasing transparency about how Web services use data, tools like XRay increase user awareness and, potentially, pressure on services to behave responsibly. She noted that the tool could also be of use to privacy watchdogs, such as the Federal Trade Commission (FTC), and investigative journalists.

She pointed out that the algorithms used to analyze online data can unintentionally lead to harmful, unintended, and/or unanticipated consequences, such as price discrimination. Her group has also created an infrastructure called FairTest to help programmers identify privacy bugs in their applications, enabling them to avoid discriminatory or other unintended effects. Geambasu suggested that the strategies embodied by these tools for enhancing online privacy could be applicable to privacy protection in other domains.

Steven M. Bellovin noted that there are many definitions of privacy. He identified one of the most common definitions as the ability to control what happens to one's personal information. Based upon this definition, he identified the following two key types of privacy offenses: (1) using data for a purpose other than that for which they were originally collected and (2) linking data from two or more different sources. He noted that the second type of offense is a specific instance of the first.

He illustrated the first offense with the example of driver's licenses, which are intended to indicate that an individual is legally qualified to drive, but are used secondarily for boarding airplanes or entering bars. He pointed out that many bars scan driver's licenses to verify their validity, and some actually record a patron's name, address, and demographic data, which may itself constitute a privacy violation.

Bellovin went on to discuss privacy issues related to biometrics data, including fingerprints or facial patterns. He pointed out that it is difficult to control the secondary use of biometric information. For example, an individual's image could be obtained or captured without his or her knowledge in a public place, then matched to other sources. If linked to an individual's Facebook profile, personal information about that person can be obtained, whether directly or through data analytics; for example, a student project from the Massachusetts Institute of Technology (MIT)[1] showed that one can accurately infer an individual's sexual orientation by analyzing that person's Facebook network. Bellovin noted that compromised data from the recent Office of Personnel Management (OPM) breach includes information that could potentially be linked to Facebook photos, leaked records from Ashley Madison, or other data sources to reveal sensitive information even if the other data sources contain no personally identifiable information (PII). This underscores the fact that privacy issues can arise even in the absence of PII. Even without a user's name, a Web service such as Netflix or Amazon can build a dossier for that user. Health records, even in the absence of PII, are still extremely personal and can be re-identified.

---

[1] C. Jernigan and B.F. Mistree, 2009, Gaydar: Facebook friendships expose sexual orientation, *First Monday*, 14(10).

He suggested that biometric data, when linked to other sources, present tremendous potential for privacy violation. He proposed that using salted hashes of biometric data might be more privacy-preserving than direct use of biometric data such as a facial image or a human fingerprint.

James Wayman discussed two major themes: (1) meaning derived from the absence of information and (2) the privacy of members of the IC.

He began by pointing out the idea from Zen philosophy that the empty space between objects is just as important as the objects themselves. He carried this into the intelligence field, noting that the utility of information is often inverted from what one might expect. Sometimes the absence of information reveals a lot, as when "listening in the gaps" between pieces of information during the intelligence practice of traffic analysis. Wayman provided a specific example: Fugitive terrorists may likely be off the grid, meaning that they may be the ones for whom no communications data exists. He suggested that the IC would like to do more data reduction, but persists with data retention because it is hard to know what to throw away when the ability to recognize the absence of signal may also be important.

He also suggested a need to consider not only the emerging IC technologies that could threaten privacy, but also how emerging technologies threaten the privacy of members of the IC.

PANEL DISCUSSION

Unintended Consequences of Data Collection and Use

Bellovin suggested that unintended consequences often arise in the context of secondary use. He recalled a statistic suggesting that commercial data brokers may have more than a thousand data points on the average American. Secondary use of data can lead analysts to draw spurious conclusions from observed correlations. Incorporating such conclusions into hiring decisions or insurance qualifications could have unfair and detrimental consequences.

Geambasu suggested that unintended consequences may become increasingly significant as we move into a data exchange-based world. Primary- and third-party-collected data is obtained by fourth-parties—data brokers—with whom users may never interact. Data brokers hold vast quantities of data about users, the flow of which cannot be effectively tracked or managed.

Wayman noted that the U.S. VISIT[2] program, through which the U.S. government collects biometric information about foreign visitors to the country, led other nations to collect biometric information from non-national travelers. This, combined with the leak of fingerprint records from the recent OPM breach, could have significant consequences for those within the intelligence community.

Wayman also addressed the unintended consequences of the *absence* of data in a data-rich world. He noted that people who turn off their phones when entering an IC facility to avoid tracking might inadvertently raise a red flag. Bellovin highlighted an example from World War II, when the research of U.S. nuclear physicists ceased to be published, tipping off the Soviets that their work had been taken out of the public eye.

Emerging Technologies with Potential Consequences

Panelists identified the technologies whose privacy implications they found most worrisome.

Bellovin noted that he was most concerned about the potential privacy implications of remote (or involuntary) capture of biometric information, and those of machine learning, which can already arrive at sensitive correlations—and these technologies continue to advance.

Gunter reiterated his concerns around the convergence between health care and health technologies. For example, in the health care sphere, the security of a wirelessly controllable defibrillator is scrutinized by

---

[2] This program has been superseded by the Office of Biometric Identity Management program, enacted in 2013.

regulators, but that of a fitness monitor like Fitbit is not. He worries that the incentive to add capabilities to lower-end products could lead to a host of insecure mid-level products, such as an insulin pump that transmits information to—or is even controlled by—a mobile phone, bringing with them significant security and privacy risks.

Wayman pointed out that iris recognition at a distance, kick-started through the Defense Advanced Research Projects Agency's Human Identification at a Distance program, is already commercially available and can work at a distance up to approximately 10 feet. The Intelligence Advanced Research Projects Agency's Janis project is currently focusing on improving facial recognition under a variety of different conditions.

The Evolution of Multiparty Interaction with Data

Geambasu pointed out that the online data landscape is complex, and information is tracked by many agents on a variety of websites. Whether or not these trackers know a user's name, they may have information about other sites a user has visited, or even other devices used, and may exchange cookies with others. Neither users nor researchers fully understand this landscape, and all that can currently be done is to try to break the black box around such exchange. She noted that one (possibly controversial) solution would be to make such exchange of data explicitly legal and then devise an infrastructure that would ensure rigorous compliance with a set of appropriate controls.

Gunter added that there are similar issues around the architecture of advertising on mobile phones. Specifically, on Android phones, an app's advertisers can have the same privileges as the app itself. It is thus possible for an advertiser to access a phone's microphone or camera, the effects of which some have been trying to measure. There is a large potential for harm in this space; advertisement-supported apps are quite popular because they tend to be free, but advertisers may have access to sensitive data, such as medical information, collected by the apps themselves.

Bellovin reiterated the extent of online tracking, referring to a statistic that as much as 40 percent of people's Internet bandwidth goes to trackers and ads. He agreed that it is difficult even for a knowledgeable person to understand where his or her information is going.

He noted that the Fair Information Practice Principles (FIPPs) instantiated in the Privacy Act of 1974 do not apply to the IC, and that U.S. law is unclear on the circumstances under which the government can purchase data from third parties—an action that could enable circumvention of other provisions in the law. For example, under the Stored Communications Act, communications companies cannot sell or give certain information to the government. However, there seems to be no prohibition against the government obtaining this information from a data broker.

Geambasu noted that there could be value in engaging auditors to monitor and provide oversight of data practices that users cannot see. Gunter asked who the auditors might be, and noted that allowing a company or the government to perform this role would raise trust issues and potential conflicts. Geambasu pointed out that the financial sector has an established infrastructure, though it may not work perfectly, and suggested that a similar infrastructure could be established for auditing the Web.

Collection of Data about One User That Reveals Information about Someone Else

Gunter pointed out that direct consumer genomic testing results can reveal hereditary information and thus enable inference about a subject's family members. He pointed out that medical professionals have well-defined protocols for revealing the presence of genetic markers that could have dire implications for a user's family members, but there is no regulation or guidance on this in the direct-to-consumer space. It is not uncommon for an individual to post his or her entire genetic sequence online, which could have unwanted effects on family members.

Gunter also discussed a study[3] that addressed the notion of ownership of identity, describing one of its conclusions—namely, that someone who holds data about an individual actually owns that identity, whether or not it is complete or accurate. He also pointed out that an individual's own self-identity could be less accurate than the identity held by another party, because the individual might engage in self-delusion. Bellovin suggested that the findings of this study could be useful to workshop participants.

Bellovin also noted that Facebook's tagging function could enable an individual to reveal information about someone else. Coincidence of location data can also be used to infer information about an individual whose behavior is linked to that of others about whom much is known. For example, machine learning correlations within a given data set have enabled identification of marital/relationship status and ethnicity of individuals about whom only location data over time had been collected.

Geambasu also raised the example of Google Glass, which can collect information on people other than its users, including through video. This and other augmented reality technologies present significant challenges to managing privacy. She pointed out that setting data access controls with mainstream technologies such as Facebook is already difficult, and the management problem will likely increase significantly.

Industry Practice as a Potential Model for the IC

Geambasu suggested that companies such as Google have infrastructures for auditing access to data and maintaining data that are not in use, involving encryption, and minimization and compartmentalization of access. Such strategies, along with anonymization of data moving between services, could be a good model.

Bellovin pointed out the value of minimization: If data do not exist, they cannot be abused. Geambasu agreed, but also pointed out that some data holders keep seemingly unnecessary data in case they might be useful in the future; these parties can take other strategies to separate and sequester data that are not currently valuable to reduce the risk of misuse.

Gunter proposed the idea of developing abstract frameworks that could allow analogies between different sectors. For example, this could enable an understanding of how people feel about privacy with respect to smart electric meters to inform strategies for managing privacy in connected vehicles. He noted an idea, from a recent workshop related to intelligence, of creating a framework that distinguishes data collection from data use—an idea that has not been emphasized in other sectors.

Bellovin pointed out that a recent President's Council of Advisors on Science and Technology report[4] emphasized controls on data use rather than on collection. He noted that some privacy advocates are uncomfortable with this, because even the best use control policies can be changed in ways that open up pathways for unintended or harmful use of stored data.

Defining Privacy

Wayman referred to the idea that "privacy is a concept in disarray"; people struggle to articulate its meaning.[5] He shared an anecdote from past work on an International Organization for Standardization committee for terminology development where a representative pointed out that there is no single word for privacy in Russian. Wayman suggested that it could prove fruitful to focus instead on more carefully

---

[3] National Research Council, 2003, *Who Goes There: Authentication Through the Lens of Privacy*, Washington, D.C.: The National Academies Press.

[4] President's Council of Advisors on Science and Technology, 2014, *Big Data and Privacy: A Technological Perspective*. Washington, D.C., https://www.whitehouse.gov/sites/default/files/microsites/ostp/PCAST/pcast_big_data_and_privacy_-_may_2014.pdf.

[5] D.J. Solove, 2006, A taxonomy of privacy, *University of Pennsylvania Law Review*, pp. 477-564.

articulated rights. He pointed out a recent academic paper discussing a "theory of creepy."[6] He proposed that whether or not a practice is perceived as "creepy" could be a very useful benchmark.

Gunter suggested that privacy, like friendship or security, will never have a precise definition, and that this should not dissuade people from respecting it or thinking about it. Another participant suggested that there are many words and terms in any culture that embody facets of the values we associate with the term privacy.

OPEN DISCUSSION

Challenges around Control and Use Frameworks

One participant, picking up on the earlier discussion of controls on collection and use, suggested that reasonable limits on data collection could be impractical and difficult to define, partly because of the vast quantity and range of data that might be collected and partly because the appropriateness of collection depends on the ultimate use—which is largely unknowable. The participant wondered about the possibility of instead developing a framework for data control and use, noting that the appropriateness of control and use is situation-dependent.

The group discussed the idea of a mathematical framework that might enable objective and automated generation of limits on data use. Several participants noted recent work attempting to develop formal models of the data use rules contained in HIPAA, aiming to enable computers rather than attorneys to make data-sharing decisions. One participant noted that researchers had found holes in this approach. One of the panelists suggested that there are no general concepts of use that are immediately and universally applicable; every concept of use would require its own ontology to achieve a context-specific meaning.

A participant identified some of the limitations of restrictions on use:

1. They are difficult to enforce, and enforcement depends upon generally under-resourced enforcement agencies.
2. Because restrictions are generally imposed only after something bad has happened, they are thus more punitive than preventative.
3. Use restrictions may be subject to attack under the First Amendment; if data were lawfully collected, what is the legal justification for limiting their use?

A panelist raised an example of advertising targeted at an individual whose online activities displayed characteristics associated with depression, pointing out that targeted advertisements could be helpful (for example, advertisements for a support group) or detrimental (for example, providing advertisements for alcohol). Someone else suggested that rather than focusing on the ethics of the outcome in this scenario, we should actually be more concerned with the ethics of conducting this level of profiling without the user's consent in the first place, whether or not there is currently a legal mechanism to restrict such profiling.

Bellovin suggested that one benchmark to consider for use restriction is whether possession or analysis of the data in question is likely to result in a data holder taking an action that he or she would not have otherwise taken. Weighing the benefits of a given use against its "creepiness" factor could be helpful.

Best Technical Practices

Geambasu proposed some important privacy practices that could be deployed at the service level:

---

[6] O. Tene and Jules Polonetsky, 2015, A theory of creepy: Technology, privacy, and shifting social norms, *Yale Journal of Law and Technology* 16.1:2.

- *Conduct extensive privacy testing* while developing large and complex applications. Privacy implications are often unintended consequences, and must be actively sought in order to be prevented. Such testing could be required by companies and conducted by programmers.
- *Manage data effectively*. If data are not being used, keep them separate and secure—even require permission all the way up the management chain before they can be accessed.

Bellovin proposed a few more practices:

- *Avoid globally unique identifiers*, which make it easy to link data across time and among different applications.
- *Avoid looking at data that are not necessary*. For example, the Outlook mail service does not read email content when selecting ads to display.
- *Do not collect data that are not needed*. If they do not exist, then they cannot be abused.

A participant noted that the discussion had centered on technologies in the context of academia and the private sector. It was pointed out that the workshop was in fact meant to help expose the IC to outside research and practice around privacy, to provide new perspectives, and to help enrich thought about privacy within the IC. This was followed by some discussion of privacy in the context of the IC.

Wayman noted that the IC is clever about using data, suggesting that any general rules about the IC's use of data could have minimal impact. He suggested that the IC does a good job of protecting individual privacies of members of the public, but that the privacy risks for those within the IC may be substantially higher.

Another participant noted that translating the FIPPs or other policies into concrete and substantive operational requirements is challenging across any industry, and suggested that technologies to help with this translation could be useful to those who design applications.

Bellovin pointed out that the FIPPs apply to the U.S. government, and have analogues in other developed nations' data protection commissions; they are not, however, broadly applicable to the commercial sector, with the exception of HIPAA. He noted that FIPPs may be rather obsolete, because they focus on identity; he reiterated that profiling and inference of sensitive information can occur whether or not a data set contains identity information. He said that part of his research centers on creating a new formal definition of privacy and the harms that result from various activities. He suggested that for the IC, privacy violations are more likely to arise when focusing on a specific person—but much of the IC's work is concerned with larger trends, rather than individuals.

Gunter added that it makes sense to think of FIPPs as a starting point, and ask how they should be extended, suggesting that looking beyond the FIPPs could be an important strategy. He also suggested that more progress could be made on privacy by drilling down to sector-specific contexts and ontologies than by focusing on high-level ideas.

5

Social Science and Behavioral Economics of Privacy—Panel Summary

REMARKS FROM PANELISTS

Frederick Chang, director of the Darwin Deason Institute for Cyber Security, the Bobby B. Lyle Endowed Centennial Distinguished Chair in Cyber Security, and professor in the Department of Computer Science and Engineering in the Lyle School of Engineering at Southern Methodist University, introduced the next panel on the topics of attitudes, preferences, and behaviors as they relate to privacy. He noted that the panel would touch on attitudinal surveys, privacy behaviors, how much people pay for privacy, and the societal impacts of privacy, informed by the panelists' backgrounds in economics, behavioral economics, computer science, psychology, media and communications, law, and information systems. Chang, as moderator, introduced the following panelists and gave each of them 5 minutes for opening comments:

- Idris Adjerid, assistant professor of management, University Notre Dame;
- Jessica Staddon, associate professor of computer science, North Carolina State University;
- Joseph Turow, Robert Lewis Shayon Professor of Communication at the Annenberg School for Communication, University of Pennsylvania; and,
- Katherine Strandburg, Alfred B. Engelberg Professor of Law, New York University.

Idris Adjerid discussed his research on the economics of privacy with a focus on behavioral economics. Through his work, he has found that privacy decision making is particularly susceptible to deviations from rational choice. This runs counter to the common assumption that people have consistent privacy preferences, make rational decisions, and act in their own best interest. He noted that there are many examples that illustrate such irrational privacy behavior.

He highlighted the specific example of the control paradox, the phenomenon where the illusion of control can be comforting. Experimental work has shown that giving users more controls puts them at ease, and makes them more willing to disclose information—whether or not the controls actually enhance benefits or reduce risk.[1] This work suggests that systematic changes can be induced in people's behavior by manipulating subtle or even insubstantial factors—counter to rational models of behavior.

One study demonstrating this effect provided a set of substantive privacy controls under different names to participants. Participants presented with the options labeled "privacy settings" were 56 percent more likely to actually use protective options compared to a group given the same options labeled "survey settings." A similar experiment suggested that perceived changes in the risk of data disclosure can have a more profound effect on behavior than the objective differences in risk.

Adjerid noted the large amount of evidence suggesting that people are bad at making privacy decisions, but also that this is not always the case. For example, a recent study out of MIT by Catherine Tucker and Alex

---

[1] L. Brandimarte, A. Acquisti, and G. Loewenstein, 2013, Misplaced confidences: Privacy and the control paradox, *Social Psychological and Personality Science* 4(3):340-347.

Marthews[2] found a measureable change in people's search behavior after the recent disclosures about intelligence collection practices. In particular, people were less likely to search certain terms on Google that previously had been identified as personally sensitive, suggesting a deliberate attempt to mask search interests.

Adjerid has examined how behavioral economics translates to consumers' decisions about themselves, with an eye to limitations and rationality. Another important topic—on which little research has been conducted—is how individuals make decisions about other people's privacy, which was touched on in the previous panel's discussion of tagging images on Facebook. It is unclear whether or not individuals will be good at managing other people's privacy and which factors affect that ability. He suggested that this question could be relevant to how individuals in the IC approach data decisions involving sensitive data about other people, and how appropriate mindsets might be systematically encouraged.

Jessica Staddon described her background in industry research, most recently at Google. She noted that she was about to begin an academic position at North Carolina State University and was not representing Google at the workshop. She focused her remarks on three main points: (1) the value of transparency, (2) privacy measurement, and (3) industry's role in the privacy ecosystem.

Like many previous panelists, Staddon emphasized the value of transparency, using insights pulled from her time in industry. She described Google Dashboard, which enables a user to see his or her own search history as tracked by Google. In the face of concerns that the information revealed through such tools might cause users to recoil and use Google less (or even close their accounts), she and her colleagues searched for any evidence that such transparency tools would have a negative effect. They found none. To the contrary, researchers found many positive associations between the use of these tools and feelings of trust and control, based on direct user feedback. She noted that, in general, data owners should be thinking about how to return some value or utility to the users from which the data were derived, and that transparency is one way to provide such utility.

Staddon then discussed challenges surrounding privacy measurement. She noted that many in the privacy research community have been pushing for the same kinds of standards that are found in the hard sciences—more of a culture of repeatability, with more consistency of measurement techniques and more objective measurements. Staddon has found that many research findings are inconsistent—for example, she knows of some very solid papers that find no difference in privacy concerns between genders, and some very solid papers that do. There is also a wide variation in reported rates of concern around certain privacy topics.

She noted that we have a poor knowledge of historical trends. Many questions will be hard to answer without some consensus and some means for documenting privacy incidents. For example:

- Are privacy incidents becoming more common?
- What is the most common cause of such incidents?
- How do these trends vary by geography, or by demographics?

She suggested one source for such data could be a crowd-sourced but moderated (along the lines of Wikipedia) privacy data repository where people could report and document events.

Finally, Staddon expressed concern about the privacy ecosystem—especially the role of industry, which is a huge player. She noted that industry holds a huge amount of data about privacy preferences and behaviors and suggested that it needs to be a part of the conversation, and also needs to work on innovations for privacy. She has heard anecdotes suggesting that many companies are becoming increasingly risk averse when it comes to research and development that could lead to privacy innovations, likely due to regulatory barriers to conducting such research and the potential that findings about the privacy implications of their own practices could result in more scrutiny from oversight bodies.

---

[2] A. Marthews and C. Tucker, 2014, "Government Surveillance and Internet Search Behavior," March 23, available at SSRN 2412564, https://papers.ssrn.com/sol3/papers.cfm?abstract_id=2412564.

Joseph Turow described the two major thrusts of his research. He has long studied how companies deal with digital relationships and issues of surveillance, particularly in the marketing and retailing sectors. Since 1999, he has also worked on approximately ten national surveys conducted through major research companies. He went on to summarize some of his basic findings.

First, people generally know that their online activities are being tracked—this is apparent from a range of surveys, as well as from anecdotal reports.

Second, there is nonetheless a huge ignorance about the details of what goes on in the digital arena. For example, people think the government is protecting them more than it actually does. This has been observed around phenomena such as price discrimination. At least two surveys have suggested that people think it is illegal for companies to charge different people different prices for the same goods. Turow suggested that such ignorance is not because people lack intelligence but because they are busy and simply do not have the time to examine and interpret the complicated information that exists about such protections.

Third, there is evidence that people philosophically do not like trade-offs. In one of his recent surveys[3]

- 91 percent of respondents disagreed with the statement that receiving a discount is a fair exchange for companies collecting their data without their knowledge;
- 71 percent disagreed with the statement that it is fair for a store to monitor their online activity while shopping there, in exchange for free access to the store's Wi-Fi.
- 51 percent disagreed with the statement that it is okay for a store to use the information it has about them to create a picture of them that would help to provide them with better service.

Nonetheless, many firms say that people accept trade-offs.

In their report on this survey,[4] Turow and his coauthors argue that it is not the case that people consent to giving away their personal information in exchange for some benefit; on the contrary, the evidence suggests that Americans are simply resigned to having their data taken.

He noted some specific findings from the study:

- 84 percent of respondents agreed that "I want to have control over what marketers know about me."
- 65 percent of respondents agreed that "I have come to accept that I have little control about what marketers know about me."
  — 58 percent agreed with both of these statements.
- 72 percent of respondents disagreed with the statement that "What companies know about me online cannot hurt me."
  — 41 percent of respondents fell into all three of these categories.

Turow said these findings imply that something serious is going on. He suggested that it's not just people who are suspicious, but companies as well. He recalled a conversation with a contact from a major retailer who was concerned that large Internet companies could share information about customer activities with the retailer's competitors.

He concluded by noting that these findings and anecdotes raise many interesting questions about harm and public perceptions. He suggested that these findings could relate directly to how people view the IC.

Katherine Strandburg focused her remarks around two themes: (1) intrinsic failures of any online privacy market and (2) the social value of privacy. She began by arguing that any idea of an online privacy market fails because it fails to accurately reflect consumer preferences. In general, markets enhance social welfare because transactions reflect consumer preferences—people are willing to pay what the product is

---

[3] J. Turow, M. Hennessy, and N. Draper, 2015, "The Tradeoff Fallacy: How Marketers Are Misrepresenting American Consumers and Opening Them Up to Exploitation," Annenberg School for Communication, University of Pennsylvania, June, https://www.asc.upenn.edu/sites/default/files/TradeoffFallacy_1.pdf.

[4] Ibid.

worth—and this is a good thing. However, in the case of privacy, consumers do not know what price they're paying when their personal data is being collected.

She reiterated Turow's point that the fact that consumers acquiesce to the collection of their personal data does not accurately signal their preferences. She said that there are many reasons consumers do not understand the price of giving up their own data, including (1) information asymmetry and (2) behavioral economics factors. She emphasized that the most fundamental problem with the idea of price in this context is that the incremental cost to a consumer of giving up data depends on what data about them is already out there and what data about them will be disclosed in the future by anyone. She said that the price or cost of giving up any single piece of data in any single transaction is thus effectively unknowable, so the idea of a privacy price is meaningful only in aggregate. The same is true when considering the value to an individual consumer of a given privacy-protecting alternative—the consumer does not know whether the information could be obtained anyway through some other means.

Strandburg introduced the possibility, in line with the results of Turow's study, that consumers treat online activity as an all-or-nothing proposition: They choose to be online and risk compromising their privacy, or else they choose not to be online and lose the value of the Internet. She suggested that this could explain the so-called paradox that people expose their data online even though they say they care about privacy. This would mean that we are in a bad equilibrium where it is hard for an individual to switch out of a market with a host of useful services that are accessible only by giving up one's data. Such a change would require collective action; it does no good to make a partial switch to a privacy protective service. Given the barriers to change, data collection persists even when consumers would prefer an alternative system.

Strandburg then pointed out that privacy is not only an individual value, and that online privacy markets, consent-based systems, or even democratic voting systems do not necessarily account for the social value of privacy. She went on to explain that privacy may have positive externalities, such as the social benefits of individuals exploring non-majoritarian views. Another example is the network benefits of emerging technologies such as social media that are not taken into account by individuals; surveillance can have chilling and conforming effects on people and their decision-making that would inhibit these network benefits. She also pointed out that technology can change the locus of social life, and the implications of a particular surveillance can change significantly as technology changes.

Strandburg also noted that short-term benefits may be overestimated in comparison to long-term social costs, and that surveillance impacts might be undercounted because they are often concentrated in underrepresented or economically disadvantaged groups. She suggested that we need more empirical studies of the social costs and benefits of privacy, rather than just the costs and benefits for individuals.

PANEL DISCUSSION

Chang then led the panel in discussion, which centered around several topics.

Recent Examples of Tipping Points

Turow suggested that companies that have experienced data breaches, such as Target, may have lost some business in the short term, and incurred the cost of credit protection services for those who were affected, but it is not clear that they will suffer long-term consequences. He said he used to think that people would rise up and reject online tracking for marketing purposes, but the changes are incremental, and people may be so wedded to the status quo that it could take a huge "disaster" for real changes to occur. He suggested that we have not really seen such a tipping point yet in the marketing sphere.

Turow went on to agree with Strandburg's remarks that the real question is societal. He proposed that we should be thinking about the broader trajectory of society. He questioned what would happen in the absence of visible tipping points. Chang and Turow suggested that it is not so much about tipping points as it is about the changing sense of what is normal, and how that impacts society.

Adjerid agreed that there is probably not a single identifiable event that marks a tipping point for privacy concerns at the societal level. He suggested instead that there may be a series of mini-events that, depending upon how they are presented, could result in individuals experiencing tipping points. He provided an example of a recent study in which privacy-relevant information was presented in a salient way to mobile users. In one instance, being told that a particular app leaked location information thousands of times in a single day was a significant point for individual users. He suggested that, rather than experiencing some exogenous societal shock, individual members of society experience their own personal tipping points. However, over time a critical mass may change their perspective, resulting in a societal push to respond to a certain practice.

Staddon added that the flood of re-identification of purportedly anonymous databases (e.g. of publicly released AOL search logs and Netflix customer rental data), has changed attitudes—but so far seems to have produced resignation rather than calls to action. Turow suggested that the Ashley Madison breach could be a tipping point for a subset of the population.

Strandburg suggested that the Snowden disclosures might have been a tipping point with respect to the IC—though it may be too soon to say—akin to the revelations that led to the Church committee investigation and subsequent reforms. Invoking her background in physics, Strandburg suggested that we are arguably in a metastable situation, from which it can be difficult to return to an optimal situation, even through tipping points.

Anticipating Future Tipping Points

Turow recommended caution when thinking about how attitudes and behaviors will change across time, in particular while considering generational differences. Many have suggested that millennials think differently about privacy than members of older generations, but some of Turow's research shows that the thinking is not as different as one might imagine. He also suggested that an individual's attitudes might change over time.

Adjerid voiced concern about the risks of relegating privacy protection to a notice-and-consent paradigm (where users are provided a sometimes overwhelmingly complex privacy policy to which they must consent in order to use a service), as it puts the burden on users while avoiding some of the hard questions around what uses are appropriate or inappropriate. He also noted that the IC does not have this luxury. He suggested it will not be easy to tell how quickly we might approach a tipping point around this model.

Strandburg suggested that we might start seeing tipping points as awareness and concern about equality issues increase. People may feel less resigned or have different expectations around equality. Turow agreed, and noted that he is finding more and more concern about equality in the retail space. But he also noted that Americans have come to accept many hierarchies and inconveniences, such as airline boarding protocols and luggage restrictions, which he referred to as the "gerbilization" of life. He pointed out that, in general, no one stands up and complains, but suggested that inequality in the application of certain inconveniences could lead to a tipping point.

Turow also expressed concern that some parties might attempt to make people believe they can have control over their information without actually providing significant controls, a practice he referred to as "pseudo-transparency." For example, an app may ask for permission to use your location data without telling you that it plans to sell the data to other companies. Publicity about pseudo-transparency could make people very angry.

Improving Trust

Adjerid suggested that concerns about data misuse—or perceived misuse—could be assuaged by demonstrating how individuals within an organization can make the right decisions in a context where there is not a clear right and wrong. He then discussed some research on how individuals make decisions about other people's privacy describing some early but interesting findings related to the roles of reciprocity and social norms. He has found that most individuals say they are respectful and cognizant of others' privacy, but fewer say that other people are respectful and cognizant of their privacy. This could be due to a disconnect between the ways we perceive how considerate we are versus how considerate other people are. Another possible explanation is that any visible bad actor skews an individual's perceptions of others.

Adjerid is also examining whether "niceness" is a predictor of cognizance of another's privacy, by evaluating results in terms of where respondents fall on the psychopathy spectrum. His early results suggest that there is no significant difference; psychopathy did not have a moderating effect. Most people, including "nice" people, are more willing to disclose sensitive information about other people than about themselves, which suggests that the role of individual judgment in grey-areas is not straightforward.

Adjerid suggested that similar arguments can be made about individual decision-making around norms in an institutional setting. Individuals may impose—even subconsciously—their own perceptions about the proper trade-offs between security and privacy for the people whose data they are working with. This could potentially happen in the IC, and does happen in private organizations.

Staddon added that she sees similarities between large Internet companies, such as Google, and the IC. She recalled comments from previous panels that it is difficult for an outsider to really know what the IC does. She suggested that simply being more open might help—for example, about the utility being returned to the public, the types of things that are being studied, or even the fact that thought is going into these decisions. This would come with risks. People might try to poke holes in the chosen practices, or ask questions that the IC cannot answer—but more openness could still have significant benefits.

Strandburg suggested that trust could be improved by being more transparent about the efficacy of the IC's privacy protection practices. She also noted that her interactions, though somewhat limited, with people in the IC suggest to her that there is a very high degree of professionalism in the community. Instilling certain ethical attitudes as part of the professional identity of a community can be important, in particular for the IC.

Turow added that he thinks the public wants to see evidence that their information is being handled with respect. He suggested that, before the recent disclosures about intelligence practices, Americans gave more credit to the government than to marketers when it came to privacy but that this attitude has probably changed. He also noted that there is no simple recipe for building trust. It will be an incremental process, during which the community must demonstrate a genuine respect for the larger society. It will take a lot of time.

Alexander Joel, civil liberties protection officer, ODNI, responded to some of the panel's remarks. He noted that the ideas for building trust were consistent with the IC's new efforts. In particular, the IC has principles of intelligence transparency that they are working hard to implement. He also recognized the need to be more transparent about the utility of the IC, because people's attitudes about a particular service or trust relationship depend in part on the value that it provides them. It is much easier to see such value with online services (for example, a Web service remembering a customer's preferences) than with the IC.

He also reiterated the idea of professionalism and ethics, and noted the published principles of professional ethics for the intelligence community,[5] including sections on mission, truth, lawfulness, integrity, stewardship, excellence, and diversity. The section on lawfulness reads as follows:

> We support and defend the Constitution, and comply with the laws of the United States, ensuring that we carry out our mission in a manner that respects privacy, civil liberties, and human rights obligations.

Joel pointed out that the research on how people feel about their own privacy vs. that of other people, addressed by Adjerid, has obvious relevance to the community. He noted that, without a personal stake in the matter, data managers can be very rules- and compliance-focused.

---

[5] Office of the Director of National Intelligence, "Principles of Professional Ethics for the Intelligence Community," http://www.dni.gov/index.php/intelligence-community/principles-of-professional-ethics, accessed September 8, 2015.

OPEN DISCUSSION

All participants were then invited by Chang to ask questions and discuss the points and themes presented by the panel. Chang began by asking if there is a privacy equivalent of critical security controls in the IC. Several participants pointed out that the IC has both security controls and recently published privacy controls: The privacy overlay can be found as Attachment 6 in Appendix F of Committee on National Security Systems Instructions (CNSSI) 1253.[6] The privacy controls aim to operationalize the Fair Information Practice Principles (FIPPs).

Public Perceptions and Trust

A participant noted that many in the public do not necessarily appreciate the distinction between different parts of the government, and thus do not believe that oversight of one government group by another is truly independent. The participant also pointed out that some information, including that which reflects the highest impacts of intelligence activities, is and must stay secret. The participant asked whether this undermines the IC's ability to build trust.

Adjerid suggested that demonstration of value and generation of trust are two distinct concepts. An example of demonstrating value would be telling the American public that the activities undertaken will benefit them. He suggested that a more direct strategy for building trust, one that does not necessarily require the release of secrets, is to carefully articulate what is being done to protect data.

Another participant noted that being transparent does not necessarily mean revealing everything. Nonetheless, it is not clear what kind of transparency is feasible that would make the public feel comfortable. By analogy, consider that most people do not really understand the details of how a car works, and do not need to. In order to develop trust, it may be important for the citizens to believe that the IC's goals and interests are in line with their own.

Participants discussed public perceptions of and concerns about the government's ability to access private-sector data. One participant suggested that the firewall between the data held by commercial entities and that held by the government has disintegrated and wondered what effect this had on public trust. Turow noted that his surveys had not considered this topic, but said that, in addition to the government having legal mechanisms for directly accessing company data, there is potential concern about the ability of the government to legally purchase information from an independent data broker that they would not otherwise have been authorized to access.

Another participant suggested that the challenge might actually be a lack of transparency about the meaning and interpretation of the rules and laws that govern this access. The participant noted that, while some details must remain secret, the ambiguity of oversight and governance of activities funded by taxpayers is a huge problem. One example raised was the fact that many terms, such as "targeted," used in laws such as FISA have no statutory definition. The participant found it unclear how explaining such terms could legitimately compromise the IC's mission.

Strandburg suggested that one way to understand the trust dynamic is to question whether citizens would approve of secret practices if they knew about them. One might, for instance, think about this by considering whether such practices would cause embarrassment if published in the *New York Times*. She also suggested that disclosing general ideas about what kind of data are being collected and how they are being used would help demonstrate efficacy and enhance transparency, and that there are probably things that could be disclosed without negatively impacting the efficacy or usefulness of tools.

Joel responded to several of these points to provide some perspective from the IC. First, he acknowledged the general surprise at the disclosures of how laws were being interpreted and applied, noting that the IC aims

---

[6] Committee on National Security Systems, "Security Categorization and Control Selection for National Security Systems," CNSSI No. 1253, release date March 27, 2014, https://www.cnss.gov/CNSS/issuances/Instructions.cfm.

to move forward with more transparency. He also noted that the internal process for accessing privately held data was not seen as easy within the IC, but was an elaborate process involving the Foreign Intelligence Surveillance Act (FISA) court and congressional oversight, as well as many people overseeing the process within the IC. He pointed out that there were also substantial restrictions on how any data obtained could be queried, used, and shared. Recent statistics have shown a very narrow set of uses, though an admittedly enormous collection of data. The IC supported the USA Freedom Act, which has put in place a new model with statutory transparency requirements that the community is working to determine how to implement.

A participant suggested that the question of whether secrecy undermines trust could be a good research question. Another participant noted the difference between an action being legally permitted and being acceptable to the public, and asked whether the fact that something is perceived to have value (either to the nation, to an organization, or to the public) makes it more acceptable, even if it is outside the normal boundaries of acceptability. Turow said that, in the marketing context, the public has not seen value as an acceptable justification for unwanted data practices. He had seen some evidence in the past that people would be more forgiving if the value accrued to the nation rather than to individual marketers, but was unsure of how people feel about that now. He suggested that understanding the difference between attitudes toward the government and attitudes toward corporations with respect to value and fairness are quite important, and noted that the nation might have a greater capacity for disappointing the public than a corporation might.

Adjerid described some of his work on organizations. Early findings from qualitative discussions and interviews suggest dissonance between the perspectives of higher-level and lower-level employees: Higher-level employees tended to offer the "party line" that the organization does not engage in data practices that are potentially invasive or discriminatory. Lower-level employees, such as those actually doing the data analysis, tend to find creative ways of collecting and using information that might push boundaries, but could be potentially lucrative to the organization.

Equality, Discrimination, and Consumer Profiling

A participant observed that people with different backgrounds can have very different perspectives on data collection. Strandburg reiterated that underrepresented groups can be affected disproportionately, and suggested that the government has a responsibility to those groups in a way that a company does not. She also highlighted the idea that lower-income people could be the canary in the coal mine when it comes to privacy; what gets done to those who are not very powerful could eventually become normal, and happen to us all. Turow noted that very little research has been done on the privacy preferences of certain demographic groups, such as lower-income populations and minority groups, and that this is very important to understand.

The group then discussed issues related to consumer pricing strategies. For example, loyalty programs often offer lower prices to members; this generally reflects the fact that companies gain value from tracking their members' practices. It is not clear to consumers how much companies benefit from data collection, even if the consumers see the discount. Strandburg reiterated that costs and benefits are somewhat unknowable, as they depend upon what is already known about a consumer, which will greatly influence the value of newly collected data. It was suggested that perceived injury on the part of a customer as a result of data collection is accounted for in the formula for the pricing differential.

Turow noted that loyalty programs have been increasingly used as a lure to get consumers to share data; such programs can be used in many ways. He described the current debate within the retail community about more elaborate price tailoring practices, where prices vary from individual to individual based on the profiles the company has built about each, a strategy enabled by the Internet and mobile shopping. He provided several examples to illustrate the depth of complexity we are entering into around individual profiling. At least one retailer actually gives higher prices to more loyal customers, because it is less concerned about losing their business. Some brick-and-mortar retailers have started using electronic ink, enabling them to change the price by time of day, or even tailor prices to individual shoppers. He suggested that current practices are teaching people that giving up their data is just a part of 21st century life. In 20 years, people may think that it has always been this way—indeed, no one today remembers what retailing was like in 1895. He again suggested a need to think about the consequences of these shifts for the larger society.

The group then discussed the role of experience in shaping user attitudes, motives, and incentives. According to Turow's data, fewer than 5 percent of Americans report having been directly harmed as a result of their data having been used. Turow pointed out that we are still at the beginning of the digital age. He recalled testifying in a 1985 hearing on program-length commercials, where companies were creating shows aimed at marketing toys to children, and suggesting that action would need to be taken at that time, or else people would take such practices for granted. He pointed out that today, there is a whole channel run by Hasbro.

Turow suggested that data collectors, especially the IC, are stewards of much of American society. He posed a question: "How do we want our grandchildren to think about the way the world is?" He suggested that we are really only at the beginning—that the pace of data collection and use is accelerating, and things could change rapidly.

Privacy Research

The group also discussed challenges to conducting innovative privacy research.

Staddon pointed out that the heavy public scrutiny of Internet companies creates a disincentive for companies to carry out research or make data available to researchers. In particular, if results can be interpreted as showing that a company's priorities are at odds with consumer privacy, things will become more difficult for the company. Another participant pointed out that this is a big loss, because Internet companies often have access to massive data sets that could help advance our understanding, whereas academics tend to work with small data sets.

Another participant pointed to difficulties around the study of behavior, and noted that it is easy, even for social scientists, to come to the wrong conclusions when interpreting observed behavior. For example, a lack of action on the part of an individual could indicate resignation rather than acceptance. Similarly, survey results can be off if questions are not asked in the correct way. Finally, people do not necessarily behave logically, which might reflect self-contradiction or some other factor such as resignation. The participant asked whether we are getting better at using this type of research to understand what people really care about.

Staddon noted that there are many survey practices that can provide confidence in results, such as phrasing survey questions in ways that will help to avoid bias. She noted that the community as a whole is doing more work on behavioral data. She referred to a recent study[7,8] that examined what information users were willing to share with an anonymizing filter and without one; this approach provides a better understanding of the context in which users are comfortable disclosing information. Nonetheless, we still do not know how to identify privacy-concerned users simply based upon their online behavior.

A participant asked if we really know whether individuals are being honest in their responses to surveys about privacy preferences. Turow described some of the steps his team took to address this issue, including hiring experienced public polling firms to conduct the surveys, and asking some of the same questions longitudinally. He noted that responses have been consistent and stable over time. He noted that other interpretations of such consistency are possible—including the possibility that individuals provide the answers they think the questioners are hoping to hear—but he finds this unlikely. He has compared past

---

[7] S.T. Peddinti et al. 2015, Understanding sensitivity by analyzing anonymity [guest editor's introduction], *36th Symposium on Security and Privacy* 13(2):14-21.

[8] S.T. Peddinti, A. Korolova, E. Bursztein, and G. Sampemane, 2014, Cloak and swagger: Understanding data sensitivity through the lens of user anonymity, *Proceedings of the IEEE Symposium on Security and Privacy,* pp. 493-508, doi:10.1109/SP.2014.38.

results to related questions in other surveys, including some conducted by Pew,[9] and to anecdotes. For example, the findings about resignation are consistent with what is often heard anecdotally.

Another participant pointed out different approaches that can be illustrated using the example of attitudes and behavior around nutrition. Consider an individual who is aware that he has bad eating habits. One could ask about the individual's habits, what the individual would like his or her habits to be, or whether he or she finds another person's habits admirable. In general, people have principles, but do not always follow them due to factors such as weakness or time constraints. Learning what people think is the right thing could be useful, though these ideals could be distinct from what they personally want or enjoy.

Adjerid agreed that there are ways to experimentally tease out such details. One strategy is to ask participants to anticipate how they would behave in a hypothetical scenario, and then actually implement the scenario. He has found that people do not act as they had predicted they would. Research suggests that individuals overestimate their ability to behave rationally in the future while underestimating their susceptibility to influence by non-rational factors. However, he suggested that the mechanism behind such dissonance has not yet been adequately elucidated.

Adjerid identified the tendency of individuals who care about privacy to act against these interests, which he termed the "privacy paradox." He also suggested that consumers seem to have privacy fatigue—a huge breach of a company's data may not affect its sales or stock value. He wondered whether results from social science research, which might provide evidence of this fatigue, could paradoxically lead organizations to avoid taking action to enhance privacy. On the other hand, he also asked whether inaction on the part of companies could lead to a tipping point such that people stop disclosing information to retail, Internet, or telecommunications companies, which would presumably also impact the IC's ability to do its job.

He recalled the contextual nature of privacy, and suggested that it could be helpful to learn more about the contextual nature of individual rationality in making privacy decisions. This could serve as a basis for tailoring policy around privacy in ways that could align individuals' behavior with their best interests, and for providing more predictability, and thus make it easier for organizations to plan policies and react to concerns.

---

[9] Note a recent Pew study addressing Americans' attitudes about privacy in the context of government: see Mary Madden and Lee Rainie, 2015, "Americans' Attitudes About Privacy, Security and Surveillance," May 20, http://www.pewinternet.org/2015/05/20/americans-attitudes-about-privacy-security-and-surveillance/.

6

Best Practices and Ethical Approaches for Data Collection and Use—Panel Summary

REMARKS FROM PANELISTS

Fred H. Cate, C. Ben Dutton Professor of Law at Indiana University, welcomed the group back for the second day of the workshop. As moderator, he introduced the following panelists and gave each of them 5 minutes for opening comments, noting that they had been tasked with addressing a difficult set of issues:

- Jennifer Glasgow, chief privacy officer, Acxiom;
- Rob Sherman, deputy chief privacy officer, Facebook;
- David C. Vladeck, professor of law, Georgetown University Law Center, and former director of consumer protection, Federal Trade Commission; and
- Helen Nissenbaum, professor of media, culture and communication, and computer science, New York University.

Jennifer Glasgow began by providing background on her company and her work. Acxiom is a 45-year-old data company with two main lines of business. First, it collects data from public records and other sources, aggregating it and bringing it to the marketplace, both for marketing and for fraud and risk identification purposes. Second, it hosts sophisticated data warehouses for large clients in consumer-facing industries, including 50 of the top 100 companies. In short, her company is all about data, including some of what people may perceive to be scary uses of data.

She went on to discuss three key themes, as summarized below.

1. *Compliance is no longer enough.* Acxiom has a saying that has been baked into its culture: "Just because you can do it doesn't mean you should." The challenge, however, is in determining what one *should* do. This takes a multitude of approaches and techniques, and the ability to make these determinations does improve over time.

    She suggested that many of the tools and techniques available for data collection and use are probably being deployed by both the IC and the private sector, noting a synergy between what the IC is facing in terms of scrutiny and public reactions and what some in the private sector have been dealing with for a long time. She pointed out that, while there is always the possibility of legislation, gaps in the legal framework mean that both industry and agencies need to develop their own rules and to identify and adopt best practices. The company's brand and its customers' brands are at stake.

2. *Determining appropriate uses of data.* Glasgow stated that Acxiom is pushing hard for more self-regulation; it derives its own policies, as do many other large companies. In 2014, the company conducted more than 800 privacy impact assessments taking into account all of the different stakeholders. She noted that the efficacy of the process improves with experience, over time.

    She identified public relations as a key part of the process that has been underemphasized in both the commercial sector and the IC. She highlighted the importance of understanding how best to talk about privacy issues—including what to say and what not to say. It is also important to understand what your critics say about you; whether it is valid or totally off-base, you should have the ability to defend your practices and/or set the record straight—before an incident occurs, rather than after.

3. *Learning from consumers' views.* Glasgow described some of what Acxiom has learned from its consumer-facing website. The site allows consumers to register and look at the data that Acxiom holds about them for marketing purposes, and enables them to change it, including to make corrections or to falsify information. At first, the company debated whether to allow a user to input data that were, to high certainty, inaccurate. Ultimately, it decided that, since the data were used for marketing, it would be appropriate for a consumer to receive marketing materials or targeted ads intended for those with their preferred profile (e.g., a 50-year-old wanting to be seen as a 30-year-old might actually be more interested in ads aimed at 30-year-olds). She suggested that, when it comes to data use, both facts and potential outcomes must be taken into account.

Rob Sherman began by noting that Facebook's approach to privacy has evolved, and that it has learned a lot about privacy and its importance. Today, the company's touchstone is building the trust of the people it serves, because the business relies upon its users being comfortable sharing data with the service. This drives much of the company's efforts to be responsible data stewards, which involve both complying with the law and going beyond it to best meet user expectations. He noted that there are times when no direct feedback about a particular data practice is available, which can complicate an organization's mission—a challenge that the IC likely also faces.

Facebook serves approximately 1.5 billion people globally, and the fact that they do not all have the same conception of privacy poses a major challenge. Facebook has increasingly used focus groups and found individuals to have thoughtful, sophisticated, and unique perspectives on privacy. People have different concerns and reasons for wanting to protect their information.

Sherman sees the role of Facebook's privacy professionals as not only operating the business in a privacy-sensitive way, but also as empowering users to make their own choices, or "putting people first." He noted that this requires providing people the necessary tools and controls, and making them comfortable that the company is doing the right thing even if no user tool is in place.

He noted that Facebook has an internal privacy process similar to the one that Glasgow described for Acxiom. It is referred to as cross-functional, meaning that the team comprises a broad range of stakeholders, including lawyers, engineers, security professionals, and communications experts. The engineering team is involved very early in the process, so that problems are dealt with before they are "baked in," which has made "privacy review" almost synonymous with "product review." This helps to avoid scenarios where privacy questions emerge at the end of a development process that must then either be scrapped, or have an after-the-fact fix tacked on.

Sherman noted that Facebook's approach to external communication has also evolved. In the past, the company made its product decisions internally and communicated them externally later on. The company has since learned that broader external engagement, including with privacy experts and advocates, earlier in the process actually helps the company to make better decisions, and to have a better relationship with its customers.

Finally, he described Facebook's privacy process as an ongoing review. He noted that privacy challenges tend not to be static, and that expectations continue to change; even if a decision is right at the time, the company must be comfortable revisiting it if the environment or demands change.

David C. Vladeck commended other speakers for beginning with the premise that we now live in an era where law itself fails to provide adequate guidance on privacy issues. He suggested several reasons for this failure: (1) technological development has outstripped the ability of regulators and lawmakers to keep pace and (2) legal instruments often lack the clarity that is needed to make tough decisions. He pointed out that there are ongoing battles over the meaning of the Fourth Amendment and suggested that the ambiguity inherent in many legal instruments has created difficulties for everyone. He suggested that the IC has as a result been forced to rely on self-generated norms, and the challenge has been in generating and enforcing these norms in a credible way.

He made an analogy with the private sector, suggesting that trust and public perception can be critical to a company's business model. He reiterated Sherman's point that Facebook's thinking about privacy has evolved, and noted that the company now has a well-earned reputation for being respectful of privacy. He suggested that Facebook's evolution on privacy (in the wake of a 2011 FTC enforcement action that called attention to its poor privacy practices) could serve as a model for the IC's response in the wake of the Snowden disclosures.

For example, he suggested that norms need to be developed in a transparent way, with input from the public or some external validation process, and grounded in ethics- and value-based judgments of acceptable practices. He suggested that norms also need to be communicated broadly internally, and rigorously enforced; the norms themselves are valuable only if they are credible to the public, so violation of norms must be dealt with.

He suggested that the private sector may actually know more about individuals than the IC does, although the average American may not understand this. He reiterated the idea that the IC would be well-served to be more transparent about its practices, and suggested that having the public suspicious of the community would not help the IC in the long run. He noted that, in the aftermath of the Snowden disclosures, it became clear that the public had little sense of what the IC was doing. For example, it was a surprise that bulk collection was not viewed by the IC as "use"; there was a supposition that anything that was collected was used. He concluded by proposing that it is important for the IC to engage with the public about how data are being used, including the ways that could be inimical to individual welfare.

Helen Nissenbaum focused her remarks on the ethical value of privacy, political governance, and notions of freedom. She began by reiterating that constraints on the flow of information often protect individual interests, but are also valuable for society as a whole. She provided several examples of benefits to individuals that also benefit society as a whole:

- The ability for patients to speak freely and privately to physicians about health matters also serves public health interests.
- The ability for citizens to vote autonomously in democratic elections also helps to promote legitimate democracy.
- Confidentiality and privacy in tax records enables truthful financial disclosures and proper collection of funds.

She pointed out that technology can disrupt the flow of information, and people often hold onto established norms, but they do not do so blindly. Contextual norms are not arbitrary, and not made hastily; rather, they reflect a balance of needs among different stakeholders, and have been refined over time to promote different values and goals. She suggested that we should not blindly adapt our norms to accommodate new technologies, a point that also arose in previous panels. She suggested that norms emerging around new technologies must instead maintain a focus on the goals and values that inspired the preexisting ones.

Nissenbaum also addressed political governance. In this sphere, privacy (i.e. informational norms) protects and promotes important political values, including the various freedoms enshrined in the Constitution. Technologies disrupt these norms just as seeing through walls might disrupt the Fourth Amendment.

She pointed out that many post-Snowden commentaries focused on National Security Agency's bulk collection practices. Given that almost every action today is an informational action, some have asked how the intelligence agencies could *not* collect data in bulk. But critics see such collection as informational dragnets that do not reflect what we expect from government actors in the context of liberal democracies.

Nissenbaum noted that some previously proposed mitigations are persuasive (for example, requiring that collected data only be read by machines or be subject to strict use requirements), and they may even be ethically defensible given certain types of conditions and assurances. Nonetheless, she suggested that it is important to understand what is at stake in these contexts.

She also noted that privacy protects critical freedoms against government interference in various activities and aspects of our lives. Freedom can be understood as non-interference; in other words, an individual is not a free citizen if government interferes with speech, association, or living in accordance with religious faith. The philosopher Philip Pettit defined freedom as non-domination, or security against arbitrary interference.[1] In this sense, freedom means not only limiting what the powerful are permitted to do, but also reducing or eliminating their power to do it. Nissenbaum suggested that this view is relevant to both commercial and government actors; collection of data enables government and dominant commercial actors the capacity to exercise power, and the threat of action can be almost as menacing and debilitating as the action itself. Finally, Nissenbaum noted that data collection, accretion, and analytics are disruptive. She suggested that while these practices can be used for good, it is important to understand what is at stake.

PANEL DISCUSSION

The panel discussed a number of topics, including strategies for determining appropriate practices within institutions, re-use of data, resource constraints, and how to translate ethical values into practice.

Glasgow described Acxiom's privacy impact assessment (PIA) process.

- A team identifies stakeholder concerns and possible consumer risks and harms around a given project, with a proxy advocate representing consumer interests.
- Enumeration of the possible negative impacts helps to elucidate how (or whether) a given decision would be defensible in a public space.
- Projects should be re-assessed periodically to account for shifting attitudes or laws.
- Assessment is an iterative process that evolves and improves with time.

Sherman noted a few important principles to inform privacy decision-making.

- Both actual and perceived harm (including violations of privacy or trust) can be damaging to an organization's reputation.
- External consultation is valuable, and can help to provide a nuanced understanding of external expectations. This can be performed in a confidential setting.

Vladeck identified three key types of internal participants to engage in privacy-related decision-making:

1. A "Cassandra"—someone whose job it is to identify every possible thing that could go wrong,
2. Privacy officers—who can push privacy as a core value beyond simple legal requirements, and
3. An institutional naysayer—someone who truly understands the organization's mission and is also prepared to push back on the status quo and compel alternative strategies.

Nissenbaum suggested that external input on privacy decision-making is necessary, because a company or organization has a natural bias toward its own interests. She also pointed out that ethical approaches require consideration of contextual values, and how constraints on information flow would best promote the goals of a given activity.

The panel was asked to speak to decision-making around re-use of existing data. Glasgow and Sherman noted that Acxiom and Facebook conduct separate PIAs and analyses (respectively) on every proposed new use of existing data. Vladeck suggested that unvetted new uses of data are "the landmine of privacy." Approximately half of the enforcement cases he saw brought while he was in law enforcement dealt with

---

[1] Philip Pettit, 1997, *Republicanism: A Theory of Freedom and Government*, Oxford University Press, Oxford, U.K.

companies that otherwise had good data hygiene, but neglected to examine the implications of novel new uses of data.

The panel briefly discussed the personnel resources necessary for conducting privacy reviews.

- Sherman noted that Facebook has grown its personnel focused full time on privacy significantly, to about 50 full-time staff (though others on different teams also address privacy in their work). He also described a more scalable staffing model for resource-constrained organizations, in which a core group is responsible for coordination of privacy activities, with designated individuals embedded in different business units responsible for keeping track of possible privacy issues.
- Glasgow noted that PIAs at Acxiom have become procedural, and are held twice a day; this has helped to make the process relatively quick and easy. The scale is managed in part by separating and fast-tracking the smaller, simpler decisions.
- Vladeck added that some companies have a dedicated privacy officer whose job it is to handle these issues. He noted that privacy decisions are complicated, and sometimes the wrong decision is made, but someone with oversight needs to be involved.

The moderator asked the panel to comment on how ethics and cultural values are or can be translated into the decision-making process.

Nissenbaum pointed out that ethics are unlike law in that they are based in foundational principles, which can lead to different analyses and strategies, rather on than fundamental rules. For example, an ethics-driven approach could be to firmly define an explicit set of values and then evaluate whether a given action would be counter to these values. She also noted the sense in the United States that privacy is an ethical value.

Sherman noted that his company starts with a policy that reflects its values and works to communicate that policy and to respect users' autonomy, often in concrete and tactical ways, such as by allowing a user to choose who gets to see a given status update. He also noted that there is an interest in making decisions more data-driven, in part to help meet the expectations of the users who do not speak the loudest. Facebook also documents its privacy decisions and maintains them in a database, which can assist in answering individual users' questions about data use.

Nissenbaum asked how Facebook and Acxiom define a "privacy issue," pointing out that even if Facebook users can control which friends see their posts they may not want Facebook to use that information. Mr. Sherman acknowledged that such a definition is not straightforward and noted that Facebook makes use of individuals' data in order to provide services such as prioritization of Newsfeed content. He identified a privacy issue as any negative outcome that could happen as a result of the way the company collects, uses, or stores people's data. Identification of potential issues begins with legal analysis and then takes into account user expectations and alternative approaches. Glasgow defined the term as including anything that can be viewed as negative by a consumer, regulator, or client. To identify potential issues, Acxiom has organized its business around major use areas, and attached specific ethical obligations to each area.

Vladeck suggested that an organization might generate its own operational set of ethical norms and rules by first considering its mission, such as protecting citizens from harm, and then using background norms (such as the Bill of Rights) to come up with discrete norms (such as a decision not to look at citizens' data without a clearly articulated need to do so). He suggested that there are many foundational materials for generating discrete norms.

OPEN DISCUSSION

Regulations and Internal Standards

Several participants discussed drawbacks to reliance upon externally generated rules, raising the following points:

- Companies subject to external regulation often go into compliance mode, rather than trying to anticipate future needs and rule changes.
- Regulators may not anticipate new technologies or uses.
- It may not be clear how existing rules apply to new technologies.
- The responsibility for setting norms is on the regulators, rather than the actors.
- Regulators do not want to regulate too early, as this would stifle innovation, and because early business models may change.

It was suggested that there will always be a lag between technological development and the ability of regulators to define an appropriate boundary, but that this can actually be a good thing. A participant recalled an earlier theme that people tend not to be good at protecting the privacy of others, suggesting that this is an argument against self-regulation or internal privacy standards. The participant suggested that making internal rules or standards of practice available to the public would enable review by those who do not share the organization's mission. A participant suggested that organizations should always base decisions on whether a given practice would be perceived as fair or deceptive. Someone asked how this might apply to the IC. It was suggested that this should be debated in a public way.

Privacy in the Context of Organizational Missions

A participant noted that privacy is generally secondary to the main mission of commercial companies, which is profit. Though many companies are sincerely concerned about privacy, privacy considerations often also serve the primary mission by shaping customer perceptions. The participant suggested that this is not necessarily the same for the IC, whose mission can include the security of U.S. citizens in the broadest sense, read to include securing their privacy.

Another participant pointed out that the mission of the IC is to obtain information about bad actors that would not otherwise be provided to the government, for the purpose of informing policy decisions. By definition, practices such as interception of communications intrude on privacy. It is challenging to protect privacy while intruding on privacy. The need for public trust also poses the challenge of how to be transparent while still keeping secrets. While lessons and strategies from the private sector can be helpful and informative, the IC faces additional challenges.

One of the panelists suggested thinking about privacy in terms of the "appropriate flow" of information: While some of the IC's practices would be inappropriate for a private company, they might nonetheless be appropriate for preserving privacy in the context of the IC's mission; however, this reasoning should be articulated publicly. Another participant noted that some feel the IC's mission could be undermined by articulating strategies for protecting U.S. citizens that may be less popular with the IC's foreign partners.

Transparency, Oversight, and Trust

The group discussed user privacy controls and oversight over back-end data uses. It was noted that users may not have a clear understanding of how their data are and are not used. It was suggested that users may not have the time—or may not want to take the time—to understand the nuances of how data are used on the back end of any system, but that there may be other ways of communicating this to users for their own benefit. For example, the FTC and the Irish Data Protection Commissioner have audit authority over Facebook's operations, and audit reports have been made available to the public.[2,3] Whether or not users read these reports, knowledge of this external oversight is likely a comfort to users.

---

[2] Data Protection Commissioner, 2011, *Facebook Ireland Ltd: Report of Audit*, December 21, https://www.dataprotection.ie/documents/facebook%20report/final%20report/report.pdf.

A participant noted that the IC is subject to outside (though still governmental) oversight, in particular through its own dedicated civil liberties and privacy offices and from the Department of Justice, neither of which are necessarily visible to the public. The participant asked what the community could do to build trust with the public. One of the panelists suggested that a good public relations campaign would be needed to effectively teach the public about the existing oversight mechanisms. Another of the panelists agreed, and suggested that the problem is not necessarily *what the IC is doing*, but possibly the fact that *people do not understand what the IC is doing*. The panelist suggested that the IC should be commended for the processes it has undertaken, but that it also needed to address public misperceptions. It was again pointed out that perceptions can be just as damaging as reality.

A participant suggested that a straightforward media appearance could help communicate the IC's mission and challenges to the public. Another participant suggested that this on its own would not be enough, but that there is a directed effort under way for enhancing transparency. A panelist agreed, suggesting that a sea change is needed, and noting (from experience in the private sector) the importance of education, communication, consistency, and awareness within an organization, along with publicizing the remediating actions taken in response to a privacy breach or incident. Over time, an organization learns what to say, and who should say it, given the audience. Building trust requires an ongoing commitment to a culture of both internal and external communication.

Another panelist noted that some in the public perceive a gap between the IC's public-facing commitments and its practices, noting that strategy for communicating actual practices can influence this perception. In addition, the panelist noted that the audience is diverse and could be divided up into many different subgroups, for example, U.S. and non-U.S. audiences.

A participant noted that, while the laws that govern the IC's actions are public, their meanings or interpretations are not, and some terms in the statutes are not clearly defined. In particular, many were surprised about some of the Foreign Intelligence Surveillance Court's interpretations of law. Another participant agreed, and suggested that there is a process problem, rather than a compliance problem, which could be addressed by involving adversarial viewpoints in the process, both internally and externally. It was pointed out that the IC recognizes this, and is making transparency a priority.

The group discussed the private sector's strategies for compliance with the data protection laws of different nations. Sherman noted that Facebook is structured around two data controllers, Facebook, Inc. and Facebook Ireland, with different regulators. The company also consults with other authorities. It aims to comply with all applicable laws in such a way that the user experience and protections are consistent across the board, regardless of what region the user lives in, although this is not always possible. For example, Facebook developed a Download Your Information tool in response to European Union requirements, but has made it available to U.S. and other users as well. In the case of Acxiom, products are rolled out on a country-by-country basis, and product PIAs are performed independently for each country, according to Glasgow.

Panelists concluded the session with a few comments about future strategies and the outlook for improving privacy.

Sherman said that it is important for organizations to stay humble and listen to the privacy concerns of those that they serve. He suggested that understanding and protecting privacy is an iterative process that requires persistent engagement and honest exchanges of view. The biggest challenge is that the landscape is not static, and organizations must be willing to revisit, adapt, and improve their practices. While current laws are a baseline, it is unlikely that they will predict upcoming technology changes, so continuous evaluation is needed.

Glasgow suggested that an organization should not expect perfection, especially in its early privacy strategies. Regardless of the success of any individual action, persistence is necessary to make significant progress on building trust. She also suggested that the private sector may begin to face some of the same challenges that the IC has experienced as big data and machine learning continue to pervade business strategies and the concept of notice and choice breaks down.

---

[3] Data Protection Commissioner, 2012, *Facebook Ireland Ltd.: Report of Re-Audit*, September 21, https://dataprotection.ie/documents/press/facebook_ireland_audit_review_report_21_sept_2012.pdf.

Nissenbaum suggested that society is already on a path that has strayed from ethical activity; we seem to accept that massive collection and aggregation of data is the proper state of affairs, despite the absence of a rigorous argument for why this is defensible. She noted that it is hard to turn back the clock, but suggested that there might nonetheless be value in revisiting this acceptance.

7

Wrap-Up—Panel Summary

Members of the workshop steering committee and workshop participants reflected upon key themes that had arisen during the panel discussions, and identified a few additional concepts, as summarized below.

Susan Landau reiterated Jessica Staddon's comment that the power of transparency should not be underestimated and also suggested that the accuracy of the information shared is critical to an organization's credibility. She noted that transparency can be a challenge for the IC because many details of their operations are necessarily classified, suggesting that this makes it even more important for the IC to get the big picture right when communicating with the public. For example, she noted that inconsistency in the reported number of instances in which the use of metadata was critical for the IC had undermined the community's credibility. Landau said that her experience with the Academies study on bulk collection of signals intelligence,[1] showed her how seriously the IC takes the rules around data collection, access, and use. She pointed out that this is generally not clear to those on the outside, and could be better communicated through deeper engagements with the academic community. While there are complexities associated with control of data flow and use, she suggested that better funding for privacy enforcement activities in general would be beneficial.

Tadayoshi Kohno pointed out that the absence (or perceived absence) of knowledge of IC activities among those in academia and the private sector made some of the privacy discussions challenging. He pondered the potential for developing "toy problems"—scenarios designed to embody some of the challenges that the IC faces at a classified level but without actually revealing classified or restricted information—to enable academic and industry researchers to better understand and make progress on some of the IC's privacy challenges.

Kohno noted that, because time was limited, the workshop discussions of emerging technologies were not comprehensive. He pointed out that opportunities for discussing and learning about emerging technologies could also be found at other venues, such as the annual Consumer Electronics Show or through interactions with venture capital firms.

He reiterated Mark McGovern's point that the audacity of new technologies makes it hard to anticipate their privacy implications. He pointed out that this is likely also true for any audacious new capabilities the IC might develop. He identified the recurring theme that a system's privacy must be considered from conception to deployment, and take into account evolving uses and stakeholder needs. He identified the analogous need to continuously consider privacy throughout the IC's activities, along with the public's perception of this need. Finally, he pointed out the recurring theme of how difficult privacy is to define.

Frederick R. Chang expressed a hope that this workshop might serve as a tipping point and help seed important discussions, solutions, and identification of privacy challenges to be solved. He noted that privacy is a hard problem, confounded by human irrationality, uncertainty, inconsistency of research results, and a lack of resources for innovation. He suggested that advancement of a "science of privacy" might help to make progress, alluding to efforts under way within the IC. In particular, workshops could identify grand challenge problems; researchers could develop data sets to be shared; students could be encouraged to study this field. Chang suggested that some of the gaps between the participants from the IC and those from academia and the

---

[1] National Research Council, 2015, *Bulk Collection of Signals Intelligence: Technical Options*, Washington, D.C.: The National Academies Press.

private sector may have narrowed today, and that additional meetings such as this one would provide even more added value.

Helen Nissenbaum observed that the Snowden disclosures were an eye-opener for those working on privacy, in part because they clarified the importance of compliance with the law and internal policies, but also because the public's strong reaction made it clear that people had actually expected more than just compliance.

She found that this meeting helped to start teasing out the intersection between technology, intelligence practices, and all of the values that are gathered together under the term privacy. She noted that the emerging technologies that define what the IC can do also define what everyone else can do, and that understanding how technologies change the world and the flow of information will enable everyone to be more intelligent and understanding about what should and should not be allowed to take place.

Fred H. Cate echoed and elaborated upon a number of points that arose in the panel discussions:

- *The law is not enough for protecting privacy,* and it has become less sufficient over time. Industry has had to come to grips with this.
- *Privacy is hard— but not impossible.* Important (if imperfect) steps can be taken to make a difference.
- *Transparency makes a difference.* This is difficult for the IC, but, again, not impossible. The IC can articulate its values and its commitment to accountability, including a visible commitment to firing individuals who do not live up to those values.
- *"Transparent" need not mean "public."* The use of advisory boards or councils can convey message, values, and activities in a controlled way.
- *Transparency also plays an important role in perception.* If people feel comfortable with things they know you are doing, they are more likely to give you the benefit of the doubt on the things that are not made transparent. Many companies have recognized this.
- *Rigorous data management is critical for protecting privacy.* This requires great security, appropriate responses in the wake of a breach, and building accountability into the system.
- *Creation of a value proposition can help build trust.* Being clear and straightforward about the benefits provided by the existence or use of a given data set, tool, or authority is valuable.

Workshop participants discussed these reflections and ideas, reiterated recurring themes, and added a few final reflections. There was some discussion of the IC's oversight and classification systems, with several participants suggesting a need for reform or improvements, in order to enable more transparency and assurance that privacy principles are being upheld.

Several participants discussed further the notions of an art of privacy or a science of privacy. One suggested that some sort of decision-making support tool, based upon fundamental principles, would be very helpful to organizations with limited resources for making privacy decisions, and wondered whether efforts toward a science of privacy framework might help to produce such a practical tool. Another participant recommended against the framing of an art or science of privacy, as it would seem to place the field of ethics, which provides a rigorous basis for deriving actionable principles, into the category of "art." A third participant suggested that the notion of a science of privacy might not make sense because privacy is so context-dependent.

In response to the theme that privacy is difficult to define, one participant suggested that progress might be made by addressing individual facets of privacy and its associated values, such as the following:

- The right to be forgotten,
- The concept of freedom of thought,
- The concept of freedom from physical intrusion, and

- Avoidance of being "creepy."[2]

A participant asked whether technology is upending our traditional notions of privacy. Another participant cautioned against thinking of technology as an independent force to which we must adapt, suggesting that society has a significant role—and responsibility—in shaping how technology is used.

CLOSING

Cate closed the workshop by thanking all participants, Academies staff, the workshop steering committee, and the panelists. He also thanked David Honey, director of science and technology, ODNI, Alexander W. Joel, and their colleagues from the IC for making the workshop possible. He suggested that many from academia and the private sector would be prepared to continue to engage on privacy with the intelligence community.

---

[2] O. Tene and J. Polonetsky, 2015, A theory of creepy: Technology, privacy, and shifting social norms, *Yale Journal of Law and Technology* 16.1:2, http://digitalcommons.law.yale.edu/yjolt/vol16/iss1/2/.

Appendixes

A

Workshop Statement of Task

An ad hoc steering committee will plan and convene a two-day workshop addressing the civil liberties and privacy implications of information and communication technologies. It will look at academic and industry research, emerging approaches, and best practices and consider these in the context of intelligence collection and analysis. The workshop will explore three main themes: (1) privacy implications of emerging technologies, (2) public and individual preferences and attitudes toward privacy and the social science and behavioral economics of privacy, and (3) ethical approaches to data collection and use. This workshop will involve and foster interaction between the intelligence community and academic and industry experts, and enable participants to share knowledge and active research work via presentations, panel discussions, and Q&A sessions. A rapporteur-authored workshop summary will be prepared.

B

Workshop Agenda

**KECK CENTER, WASHINGTON, D.C.
JULY 21-22, 2015**

July 21, 2015

9:00 a.m.	**Welcome and Introduction**
	Fred H. Cate, Indiana University, Steering Committee Chair
9:10	**Background and Context from the IC**
	Alexander W. Joel, Civil Liberties Protection Officer, Office of the Director of National Intelligence
9:30	**Panel I on Privacy Implications of Emerging Technologies: Mobile Communications and the Internet of Things**
	Susan Landau, Worcester Polytechnic Institute, Moderator
	Panelists: Mark McGovern, Mobile System 7
	Fuming Shih, Oracle
	Lee Tien, Electronic Frontier Foundation
	Tao Zhang, Cisco
10:20	Break
10:50	**Panel I on Privacy Implications of Emerging Technologies Mobile Communications and the Internet of Things** *(continued)*
11:50	Lunch
1:00 p.m.	**Panel II on Privacy Implications of Emerging Technologies: Biometrics, Analytics, and Health IT**
	Tadayoshi Kohno, University of Washington, Moderator
	Panelists: Steven M. Bellovin, Columbia University
	Roxana Geambasu, Columbia University
	Carl Gunter, University of Illinois Urbana-Champagne
	James Wayman, San Jose State University
2:50	Break

APPENDIX B

3:20 **Panel on Social Science and Behavioral Economics of Privacy**

Frederick R. Chang, Southern Methodist University, Moderator

Panelists: Idris Adjerid, University Notre Dame
Jessica Staddon, North Carolina State University
Katherine Strandburg, New York University
Joseph Turow, University of Pennsylvania

5:10 **Day One Wrap-Up**

Fred H. Cate, Steering Committee Chair

5:15 **Reception**

July 22, 2015

9:00 a.m. **Welcome, Outline of Day's Agenda**

Fred H. Cate, Steering Committee Chair

9:05 **Panel on Best Practices and Ethical Approaches for Data Collection and Use**

Fred H. Cate, Indiana University, Moderator

Panelists: Jennifer Glasgow, Acxiom
Helen Nissenbaum, New York University
Rob Sherman, Facebook
David Vladeck, Georgetown University

10:55 Break

11:30 **Wrap-up Panel**

Steering Committee

12:15 p.m. Adjourn

C

Biographical Sketches

WORKSHOP STEERING COMMITTEE

FRED H. CATE, *Steering Committee Chair,* is a distinguished professor and C. Ben Dutton Professor of Law at the Indiana University Maurer School of Law. He is managing director of the Center for Law, Ethics, and Applied Research in Health Information, and a senior fellow and former founding director of the Center for Applied Cybersecurity Research. Professor Cate specializes in information privacy and security law issues. He has testified before numerous congressional committees and speaks frequently before professional, industry, and government groups. He is a senior policy advisor to the Centre for Information Policy Leadership at Hunton & Williams LLP, a member of Intel's Privacy and Security External Advisory Board, the Department of Homeland Security Data Privacy and Integrity Committee Cybersecurity Subcommittee, the National Security Agency's (NSA's) Privacy and Civil Liberties Panel, the board of directors of The Privacy Projects, the board of directors of the International Foundation for Online Responsibility, and the board of directors of the Kinsey Institute for Research in Sex, Gender and Reproduction. Previously, Professor Cate served as a member of the Committee on Technical and Privacy Dimensions of Information for Terrorism Prevention of the National Academies of Sciences, Engineering, and Medicine, counsel to the Department of Defense Technology and Privacy Advisory Committee, reporter for the third report of the Markle Task Force on National Security in the Information Age, and a member of the Federal Trade Commission's (FTC's) Advisory Committee on Online Access and Security and Microsoft's Trustworthy Computing Academic Advisory Board. He chaired the International Telecommunication Union's High-Level Experts on Electronic Signatures and Certification Authorities. He served as the privacy editor for the Institute of Electrical and Electronics Engineers' (IEEE's) *Security & Privacy* and is one of the founding editors of the Oxford University Press journal *International Data Privacy Law*. He is the author of more than 150 books and articles, and he appears frequently in the popular press. Professor Cate attended Oxford University and received his J.D. and his A.B. with honors and distinction from Stanford University. He is a senator and fellow (and immediate past president) of the Phi Beta Kappa Society, an elected member of the American Law Institute, and a fellow of the American Bar Foundation.

FREDERICK R. CHANG is the director of the Darwin Deason Institute for Cyber Security, the Bobby B. Lyle Endowed Centennial Distinguished Chair in Cyber Security, and professor in the Department of Computer Science and Engineering in the Lyle School of Engineering at Southern Methodist University (SMU). He is also a senior fellow in the John Goodwin Tower Center for Political Studies in SMU's Dedman College, and a distinguished scholar in the Robert S. Strauss Center for International Security and Law at the University of Texas at Austin. Dr. Chang's career spans service in the private sector, in academia, and in government, including as the former director of research at the NSA. Dr. Chang has been awarded the NSA Director's Distinguished Service Medal and was the 2014 Information Security Magazine 'Security 7' award winner for education. He has served as a member of the Commission on Cyber Security for the 44th Presidency and as a member of the Computer Science and Telecommunications Board of the Academies. He has also served as a member of the Academies' Committee on Responding to Section 5(d) of Presidential Policy Directive 28: The Feasibility of Software to Provide Alternatives to Bulk Signals Intelligence Collection. He twice served as a cyber security expert witness at hearings convened by the U.S. House of

Representatives' Committee on Science, Space and Technology. Dr. Chang received his B.A. from the University of California, San Diego, and his M.A. and Ph.D. from the University of Oregon. He has also completed the Program for Senior Executives at the Sloan School of Management at the Massachusetts Institute of Technology (MIT).

TADAYOSHI KOHNO is the Short-Dooley Professor of the Computer Science and Engineering Department at the University of Washington and an adjunct associate professor in the university's Information School. His research focuses on computer security and privacy, broadly defined, with a particular focus on computer security and privacy for emerging and consumer technologies; computer security and privacy for mobile and cloud systems; the human element in computer security systems; and computer security education. Originally trained in applied cryptography, his current research thrusts range from secure cyber-physical systems to cloud computing. Dr. Kohno is the recipient of a National Science Foundation (NSF) CAREER Award, an Alfred P. Sloan Research Fellowship, an MIT Technology Review TR-35 Young Innovator Award, and multiple best paper awards. He is a member of the Defense Science Study Group and a founding member of the IEEE Symposium on Secure Design and the USENIX Security Steering Committee. He received his Ph.D. in computer science from the University of California, San Diego.

SUSAN LANDAU is professor of cybersecurity policy in the Department of Social Science and Policy Studies at Worcester Polytechnic Institute. Dr. Landau has been a senior staff privacy analyst at Google, a distinguished engineer at Sun Microsystems, and a faculty member at the University of Massachusetts, Amherst, and at Wesleyan University. She has held visiting positions at Harvard University, Cornell University, Yale University, and the Mathematical Sciences Research Institute. Dr. Landau is the author of *Surveillance or Security? The Risks Posed by New Wiretapping Technologies* (2011) and co-author, with Whitfield Diffie, of *Privacy on the Line: The Politics of Wiretapping and Encryption* (1998, rev. ed. 2007). She has written numerous computer science and public policy papers and op-eds on cybersecurity and encryption policy and testified in Congress on the security risks of wiretapping and on cybersecurity activities at the National Institute of Standards and Technology (NIST) Information Technology Laboratory. She currently serves on the Computer Science Telecommunications Board of the Academies. A 2015 Inductee to the Cybersecurity Hall of Fame and a 2012 Guggenheim fellow, Dr. Landau was a 2010-2011 fellow at the Radcliffe Institute for Advanced Study, the recipient of the 2008 Women of Vision Social Impact Award, and also a fellow of the American Association for the Advancement of Science and the Association for Computing Machinery (ACM). She received her B.A. from Princeton University, her M.S. from Cornell University, and her Ph.D. from MIT.

HELEN NISSENBAUM is professor of media, culture and communication, and computer science at New York University (NYU), where she is also director of the Information Law Institute. Dr. Nissenbaum's work spans social, ethical, and political dimensions of information technology and digital media. She has written and edited eight books, including *Privacy, Big Data and the Public Good: Frameworks for Engagement*, with J. Lane, V. Stodden and S. Bender (2014), *Values at Play in Digital Games*, with M. Flanagan (2014), and *Privacy in Context: Technology, Policy, and the Integrity of Social Life* (2010) and her research publications have appeared in journals of philosophy, politics, law, media studies, information studies, and computer science. NSF, the Air Force Office of Scientific Research, the Ford Foundation, the U.S. Department of Homeland Security, and the U.S. Department of Health and Human Services Office of the National Coordinator have supported her work on privacy, trust online, and security, as well as several studies of values embodied in computer system design, search engines, digital games, facial recognition technology, and health information systems. Before joining the faculty at NYU, she served as associate director of the Center for Human Values at Princeton University. Dr. Nissenbaum received a Ph.D. in philosophy from Stanford University in 1983 and a B.A. (Hons) from the University of the Witwatersrand.

INVITED PANELISTS AND SPEAKERS

IDRIS ADJERID is an assistant professor of management at the Mendoza College of Business at the University of Notre Dame. His research focuses on the economics of personal information with a particular focus on the behavioral economics of privacy decision making and data ethics. Dr. Adjerid's work has been published in *Management Science*, the *IEEE Journal on Privacy and Security*, and a number of conference proceedings and has been featured in *The Wall Street Journal, Wired.com*, and several other news outlets. He received a Ph.D. in information systems from the Heinz College of Public Policy at Carnegie Mellon University, and both an M.B.A. and B.S. in business information technology from the Pamplin College of Business at the Virginia Polytechnic Institute and State University.

STEVEN M. BELLOVIN is the Percy K. and Vidal L. W. Hudson Professor of Computer Science at Columbia University, where he does research on networks, security, and especially why the two don't get along, as well as related public policy issues. In his copious spare professional time, he does some work on the history of cryptography. Dr. Bellovin joined the faculty in 2005 after many years at Bell Labs and AT&T Labs Research, where he was an AT&T fellow. He received a B.A. from Columbia University and an M.S. and Ph.D. in computer science from the University of North Carolina, Chapel Hill. While a graduate student, he helped create Netnews; for this, he and the other creators were given the 1995 Usenix Lifetime Achievement Award ("The Flame"). Dr. Bellovin has served as chief technologist of the FTC. He is a member of the National Academy of Engineering and is serving on the Computer Science and Telecommunications Board of the Academies. He is a past member of the Department of Homeland Security's Science and Technology Advisory Committee and the Technical Guidelines Development Committee of the Election Assistance Commission; he also received the 2007 NIST/NSA National Computer Systems Security Award and has been elected to the Cybersecurity Hall of Fame. Dr. Bellovin is the co-author of *Firewalls and Internet Security: Repelling the Wily Hacker* and holds a number of patents on cryptographic and network protocols. He has served on many Academies study committees, including those on information systems trustworthiness, the privacy implications of authentication technologies, and cybersecurity research needs; he was also a member of the information technology subcommittee of a study group on science versus terrorism. He was a member of the Internet Architecture Board from 1996 until 2002; he was co-director of the Security Area of the Internet Engineering Task Force from 2002 through 2004.

ROXANA GEAMBASU is an assistant professor of computer science at Columbia University. She joined Columbia in the fall of 2011 after finishing her Ph.D. at the University of Washington. For her work in cloud and mobile data privacy, she received a Microsoft Research Faculty Fellowship, a "Brilliant 10" Popular Science nomination, an NSF CAREER award (all in 2014); an Honorable Mention for the inaugural Dennis M. Ritchie Doctoral Dissertation Award in 2013, a William Chan Dissertation Award in 2012, two best paper awards at top systems conferences (2009 and 2011), and the first Google Ph.D. fellowship in cloud computing (2009).

JENNIFER GLASGOW has provided oversight of Acxiom Corporation's global public policy, privacy, and information practices since 1991. She currently directs Acxiom's global information use policy, internal compliance with legal regulations and industry guidelines, consumer affairs, government affairs, and related public relations. In 2010 she was recognized by the International Association of Privacy Professionals (IAPP) as the profession's first Chief Privacy Officer and in 2011 was IAPP's Vanguard winner, the highest recognition given by the association of over 20,000 members for her leadership, knowledge, and involvement in the profession. She is extremely active domestically and internationally consulting with clients and advising policy makers, regulators, and government agencies about the appropriate use of personal information. She has participated in numerous international efforts to influence the development of public policy, develop industry best practices, and achieve maximum harmonization across the world. Ms. Glasgow is also a regular speaker in a variety of industries, including financial services, retail, insurance, publishing, travel and entertainment, and government use of information. She is currently active on a variety of industry boards and councils and sits on the U.S. Direct Marketing Association Safe Harbor Ethics Committee and co-chairs the Mobile Marketing Association's Privacy and Advocacy Committee. Ms. Glasgow is board member for the Foundation for Information Accountability and Governance organization and sits on the advisory board for the Political and Economic Research Council and lectures at the University of Texas, Austin, George Mason University, and the University of Arkansas on the subject of privacy. Ms. Glasgow joined Acxiom after receiving a degree in mathematics and computer science from the University of Texas, Austin, and helping develop and install a criminal justice highway safety information system for the State of Arkansas. She is active with her alma mater as a member of the UT Chancellor's Council and the College of Natural Science Foundation Advisory Council. She has also been elected to the Arkansas Academy of Computing.

CARL GUNTER is a professor of computer science at the University of Illinois, where he also serves as a professor in the College of Medicine and as director for the Illinois Security Lab and the Health Information Technology Center. His interests concern security and privacy, especially in specific application domains. His recent work has centered on the electric power grid and health care. He has also contributed to research and teaching in the areas of programming languages, formal methods, and networking.

ALEXANDER W. JOEL is the civil liberties protection officer for the Office of the Director of National Intelligence (ODNI). In that capacity, he leads the ODNI's Civil Liberties and Privacy Office, and reports directly to the Director of National Intelligence. His responsibilities include ensuring that the protection of privacy and civil liberties is appropriately incorporated in Intelligence Community policies and procedures, overseeing compliance by the ODNI with privacy and civil liberties laws, reviewing complaints of possible abuses of privacy and civil liberties in programs and operations administered by the ODNI, and ensuring that the use of technology sustains, and does not erode, privacy. His appointment to this position was announced by Director John Negroponte on December 7, 2005. Mr. Joel had previously been performing the duties of that position on an interim basis. He has more than a decade of experience with privacy, technology, and national security law. He was motivated to enter public service following 9/11. He joined the Central Intelligence Agency's Office of General Counsel in October 2002, where he provided legal advice relating to intelligence activities. Prior to joining the government, Mr. Joel served as the privacy, technology, and e-commerce attorney for Marriott International, Inc., where he helped establish and implement Marriott's global privacy compliance program, including the creation of Marriott's first privacy officer position. Before that, he worked as a technology attorney at the law firm of Shaw, Pittman, Potts & Trowbridge in Washington, D.C. (now Pillsbury Winthrop Shaw Pittman), and as a U.S. Army Judge Advocate General Corps officer, with assignments that included prosecutor and criminal defense counsel. Mr. Joel received his law degree from the University of Michigan in 1987, magna cum laude, where he was a member of the Michigan Law Review. He received his B.A. degree from Princeton University in 1984, magna cum laude.

MARK McGOVERN is the CEO of Mobile System 7, an award winning enterprise security startup and the leader in identity behavior analytics. He is a respected security industry professional, with a 25-year track record developing and deploying innovative security products for different enterprises. Prior to founding Mobile System 7, Mr. McGovern was vice president of technology for In-Q-Tel, where he led security investments for the U.S. Intelligence Community. In this role, he identified, developed, and deployed emerging security technologies to address strategic enterprise needs. Mr. McGovern's investments included: ArcSight, Corestreet, SilverTail Systems, FireEye, Red Seal Systems, and Veracode. Prior to joining In-Q-Tel, he was director of technology for Cigital, Inc. He led Cigital's Software Security Group and supported Fortune 100 clientele, including Microsoft, MasterCard International, CitiBank, and the Federal Reserve Banks of Richmond, New York, and Boston. Earlier in his career, Mr. McGovern worked as an engineer for the Central Intelligence Agency. He holds a B.S. in electrical engineering from Worcester Polytechnic Institute and an M.S. in systems engineering from Virginia Polytechnic Institute and State University.

ROB SHERMAN is the deputy chief privacy officer at Facebook, where he is responsible for managing the company's engagement on public policy issues surrounding privacy, security, and online trust. Collaborating with Facebook's product teams, regulators, and other key stakeholders, Mr. Sherman works to build the company's core commitments to transparency, control, and accountability into every aspect of the Facebook service. He joined Facebook from Covington & Burling LLP, where he represented Facebook and other leading technology and digital media companies on regulatory and public policy issues relating to privacy, data security, electronic marketing and communications, and digital content. While in private practice, Mr. Sherman was recognized by Chambers USA as one of the nation's leading media regulatory lawyers.

FUMING SHIH is a senior product manager at Oracle Cloud working on the Cloud governance project. Dr. Shih graduated from the MIT Computer Science and Artificial Intelligence Laboratory in 2014. His research is about privacy and accountability for collection and uses of personal data, especially those from our connected personal devices. The work involves understanding human behavior in privacy, modeling people's preferences for disclosing personal data, and developing tools to support user-centric privacy framework. Part of his research is now seen in the privacy features implemented on Apple's iPhone.

JESSICA STADDON is joining the Computer Science Department of North Carolina State University as associate professor and director of privacy. Previously, Dr. Staddon was a research scientist and manager at Google, an area manager at Xerox PARC, and a research scientist at Bell Labs and RSA Labs. Her interests include usable security and privacy tools, trends in privacy-related attitudes, and methods for measuring and predicting privacy-related behaviors, attitudes, and risks. She serves regularly on the program committees of ACM and IEEE-sponsored security/privacy conferences and is on the editorial boards of the *Journal of Computer Security* and the *International Journal of Information and Computer Security* and the advisory board of the Association for Women in Mathematics. She holds a Ph.D. in mathematics from University of California (UC), Berkeley.

KATHERINE STRANDBURG concentrates her teaching and research in information privacy law and in innovation law and policy, focusing on the interplay between social behavior and technological change. She has authored several amicus briefs to the U.S. Supreme Court and federal appellate courts dealing with patent law and privacy issues and was invited to speak at the Privacy and Civil Liberty Oversight Board's public meeting on Executive Order 12333 in May 2014. Recent articles include "Free Fall: The Online Market's Consumer Preference Disconnect," and "Membership Lists, Metadata and Freedom of Association's Specificity Requirement." In 2014, she published the book *Governing Knowledge Commons* (co-edited with Brett Frischmann and Michael Madison). She co-leads NYU's interdisciplinary Privacy Research Group with Helen Nissenbaum. Dr. Strandburg obtained her J.D. with high honor from the University of Chicago Law School and served as a law clerk to the Honorable Richard D. Cudahy of the U.S. Court of Appeals for the Seventh Circuit. Prior to her legal career, Dr. Strandburg was a physicist at Argonne National Laboratory, having received her Ph.D. from Cornell University and conducted postdoctoral research at Carnegie Mellon University.

LEE TIEN is a senior staff attorney and Adams Chair for Internet Rights at the Electronic Frontier Foundation (EFF). Mr. Tien began working in the area of cyberlaw in 1991, developing the first successful First Amendment theory in the Bernstein/Junger crypto export control cases in the mid-1990s. He joined EFF in 2000, working on FOIA (Freedom of Information Act) and First Amendment Issues. After September 11, 2001, his emphasis shifted to electronic surveillance law, including pen/trap, the Wiretap Act, the Stored Communications Act, the Foreign Intelligence Surveillance Act, and Fourth Amendment issues. He currently focuses on privacy, surveillance, and security, managing most of EFF's legislative work in these areas. He has been part of EFF's NSA reform litigation teams since 2006. He also works on issues related to commercial privacy and security, including big data; Do Not Track, and online behavioral advertising; electronic health records; biometrics; energy usage data and the smart grid; road usage charging, congestion pricing, and vehicle-to-vehicle communication; and the Internet of Things. Mr. Tien received his undergraduate degree in psychology from Stanford University, where he was very active in journalism at the *Stanford Daily*. After working as a news reporter at the *Tacoma News Tribune* for a year, he went to law school at Boalt Hall at University of California, Berkeley. Mr. Tien also did graduate work in the Program in Jurisprudence and Social Policy at University of California, Berkeley.

JOSEPH TUROW is Robert Lewis Shayon Professor of Communication at the Annenberg School for Communication. Professor Turow is an elected fellow of the International Communication Association and was presented with a Distinguished Scholar Award by the National Communication Association. In 2012, the TRUSTe Internet privacy-management organization designated him a "privacy pioneer" for his research and writing on marketing and digital-privacy. His forthcoming book with Yale University Press explores how retailers are using mobile devices to replicate internet-like surveillance and data gathering in physical stores. He has authored 10 books, edited 5, and written more than 150 articles on mass media industries. Among his books are *The Daily You: How the New Advertising Industry Is Defining Your Identity and Your Worth* (2012); *Niche Envy: Marketing Discrimination in the Digital Age* (2006); *Breaking Up America: Advertisers and the New Media World* (1997; paperback, 1999; Chinese edition, 2004); and *The Hyperlinked Society: Questioning Connections in the Digital Age* (edited with Lokman Tsui, 2008). In 2010, the University of Michigan Press published *Playing Doctor: Television, Storytelling, and Medical Power*, a history of prime time TV and the sociopolitics of medicine, and in 2013 it won the McGovern Health Communication Award from the University of Texas College of Communication. Mr. Turow's continuing national surveys of the American public on issues relating to marketing, new media, and society have received a great deal of attention in the popular press, as well as in the research community. He has written about media and advertising for the popular press, including *American Demographics* magazine, *The Washington Post*, *The Boston Globe*, and *The Los Angeles Times*. His research has received financial support from the John D. and Catherine T. MacArthur Foundation, the Kaiser Family Foundation, the Robert Wood Johnson Foundation, the Federal Communications Commission, and the National Endowment for the Humanities, among others. Mr. Turow was awarded a Lady Astor Lectureship by Oxford University. He has received several conference paper and book awards and has lectured widely. He was invited to give the McGovern Lecture at the University of Texas College of Communication, the Pockrass Distinguished Lecture at Penn State University, and the Chancellor's Distinguished Lecture at Louisiana State University. He currently serves on the editorial boards of the *Journal of Broadcasting and Electronic Media*, *Poetics* and *Media Industries*.

DAVID C. VLADECK is a professor of law at Georgetown University Law Center, where he teaches federal courts, civil procedure, administrative law, and seminars on First Amendment litigation and privacy. He also serves as faculty director for the law school's Center on Privacy and Technology. Professor Vladeck recently returned to the law school after serving for nearly 4 years as the director of the FTC's Bureau of Consumer Protection. Before joining the law school faculty full-time in 2002, he spent more than 25 years with Public Citizen Litigation Group, a national public interest law firm, supervising and handling complex litigation. He has briefed and argued a number of cases before the U.S. Supreme Court and more than 60 cases before federal courts of appeal and state courts of last resort. He is a senior fellow of the Administrative Conference of the United States, an elected member of the American Law Institute, and an appointed member of the Academies' Committee on Law, Science and Technology. He serves on the boards of the Natural Resources Defense Council and the National Consumers Law Center. Professor Vladeck frequently testifies before Congress and writes on privacy, consumer protection, administrative law, and First Amendment issues.

JAMES L. WAYMAN received a Ph.D. in engineering from the University of California, Santa Barbara, in 1980. In 1981, he joined the U.S. Naval Postgraduate School as an adjunct and research professor of mathematics. In 1986, he became a contractor to the U.S. Department of Defense in the areas of biometrics and technical security. In 1995, he joined San José State University to head the Biometric Identification Research Center, which was named by the Clinton administration as the "U.S. National Biometric Test Center," from 1997 until 2000. He has been a member of two committees of the Computer Science and

Telecommunications Board of the Academies (*Authentication Technologies and Their Privacy Implications* and *Whither Biometrics?*) and served for 4 years on the Panel on Information Technology. He is currently vice chair of the Department of Justice/NIST Organization of Scientific Area Committees' Subcommittee on Speaker Recognition, an IEEE Distinguished Lecturer, and a fellow of the IEEE and the Institution of Engineering and Technology.

TAO ZHANG, an IEEE fellow and Cisco Distinguished Engineer, joined Cisco in 2012 as the chief scientist for Smart Connected Vehicles and has since also been leading initiatives to develop strategies, architectures, technology, and eco-systems for the Internet of Things and Fog Computing at Cisco Systems. Prior to joining Cisco, he was chief scientist and director of Mobile and Vehicular Networking at Telcordia Technologies (formerly Bellcore). For more than 25 years, he has been directing research and product development in broadband, mobile, and vehicular networks. His leadership and technical work have resulted in new technology, standards, and products. Dr. Zhang has co-authored two books, *Vehicle Safety Communications: Protocols, Security, and Privacy* (2012) and *IP-Based Next Generation Wireless Networks* (2004). He holds 49 U.S. patents and has published more than 70 peer-reviewed technical papers. He was a founding board director of the Connected Vehicle Trade Association. He has been serving on the industry advisory boards for several research organizations. He was the founding general chair and the steering committee vice chair for the international conference series CollaborateCom, which has now evolved into the IEEE Collaboration and Internet Computing Conference. Dr. Zhang is chair of the IEEE Communications Society Technical Sub-Committee on Vehicular Networks and Telematics Applications. He has been serving on editorial boards or as a guest editor for multiple IEEE and other technical journals, including the *IEEE Internet of Things (IoT) Journal*, *IEEE Transactions on Vehicular Technology*, *IEEE Journal of Selected Areas in Communications*, and the Springer *Journal of Wireless Networks*. Dr. Zhang was also an adjunct professor at multiple universities.

ACADEMIES STAFF

EMILY GRUMBLING, a program officer with the Computer Science and Telecommunications Board of the Academies, directed the Workshop on Privacy for the Intelligence Community. Since joining CSTB in 2014, Dr. Grumbling has also served as study director for the Committee on Information Technology, Automation, and the U.S. Workforce and as staff to the Academies' Forum on Cyber Resilience. She previously served as an AAAS Science and Technology Policy Fellow in the Directorate for Computer and Information Science and Engineering at NSF (2012-2014), and an American Chemical Society (ACS) Congressional Fellow in the U.S. House of Representatives (2011-2012). Dr. Grumbling currently serves as a volunteer Associate of the ACS Committee on Environmental Improvement. She received her Ph.D. in physical chemistry from the University of Arizona in 2010 and her B.A. with a double-major in chemistry and film/electronic media arts from Bard College in 2004.

JON EISENBERG is director of the Computer Science and Telecommunications Board of the Academies. He has also been study director for a diverse body of work, including a series of studies exploring Internet and broadband policy and networking and communications technologies. From 1995 until 1997, he was an AAAS Science, Engineering, and Diplomacy Fellow at the U.S. Agency for International Development, where he worked on technology transfer and information and telecommunications policy issues. Dr. Eisenberg received his Ph.D. in physics from the University of Washington in 1996 and B.S. in physics with honors from the University of Massachusetts, Amherst, in 1988.

SHENAE BRADLEY is an administrative assistant at the Computer Science and Telecommunications Board of the Academies. She currently provides support for multiple projects, including Continuing Innovation in Information Technology; Information Technology, Automation, and the U.S. Workforce; and Towards 21st Century Cyber-Physical Systems Education, to name a few. Prior to this, she served as a senior project assistant with the board. Prior to coming to the Academies, she managed a number of apartment rental communities for Edgewood Management Corporation in the Maryland/DC/Delaware metropolitan areas.

LIZ EULLER is a senior program assistant for the Academies' Board on Energy and Environmental Systems. She currently provides support for studies focused on energy technology and policy assessments. She worked previously for the Environmental Law Institute, The Wilderness Society, the Chicago Botanic Garden, and the University of Chicago Survey Lab. Ms. Euller has a B.A. in history from the University of Chicago.

D

Acronyms and Abbreviations

CNSSI	Committee on National Security Systems Instruction
CSTB	Computer Science and Telecommunications Board
EHR	electronic health record
FIPP	Fair Information Practice Principle
FISA	Foreign Intelligence Surveillance Act
FTC	Federal Trade Commission
IT	information technology
HIPAA	Health Insurance Portability and Accountability Act
HITECH	Health Information Technology for Economic and Clinical Health Act
IC	Intelligence Community
MIT	Massachusetts Institute of Technology
ODNI	Office of the Director of National Intelligence
PIA	privacy impact assessment
PII	personally identifiable information